HANNAH'S
NORTH COUNTRY

HANNAH'S NORTH COUNTRY

HANNAH HAUXWELL
with BARRY COCKCROFT

CENTURY

London   Sydney   Auckland   Johannesburg

also by Barry Cockcroft

Hannah in Yorkshire
The Ways of a Yorkshire Dale
The Dale that Died
Princes of the Plough
A Romany Summer
A Celebration of Yorkshire
Seasons of My Life
Daughter of the Dales
Hannah: The Complete Story
Innocent Abroad

Copyright © Tracestar and Hannah Hauxwell 1993

All rights reserved

The right of Barry Cockcroft to be identified as the author of this work has been asserted by him in
accordance with the Copyright, Designs and Patents Act 1988

First published in Great Britain in 1993 by
Random House UK Limited
20 Vauxhall Bridge Rd, London, SW1V 2SA

Random House Australia Pty Ltd
20 Alfred Street, Milsons Point, Sydney, NSW 2061
Australia

Random House New Zealand Ltd
PO Box 40-086, Glenfield, Auckland 10
New Zealand

Random House South Africa (Pty) Ltd
PO Box 337, Bergvlei 2012, South Africa

Principal colour photography of Hannah Hauxwell by
Mostafa Hammuri

Design by Behram Kapadia

A catalogue record for this book is available from the British Library

Filmset in Palatino and Rockwell by
SX Composing Ltd, Rayleigh, Essex
Printed and bound by Butler & Tanner Ltd

ISBN 0-7126-9844-2

Contents

Preface

A Statement of Position and Intent

I am a Northerner in the absolute sense.

A Daleswoman, born and reared in the uplands of Yorkshire . . . a plain Daleswoman, I might add, and consider myself fortunate to be so. And since I am descended from generation upon generation of like folk, you could say that the blood which flows through my veins is a distillation of all the hereditable elements that go to make a true Northerner.

This book is about people like me. And about places which are close enough to the remote, often punishing but essentially beautiful dale in which I lived and worked for well over half a century for me to feel at home in. It is only during the last five years that I have been granted the opportunity to meet these people and see the places you will read about.

You see, I was in chains to Low Birk Hatt Farm, my family home in Baldersdale and the only home I had ever known until well past pensionable age. I suppose I shall always be wedded to that place in my heart. Cruel circumstances obliged me to leave. Indeed, it is possible to suppose that I may not have survived as long as I have if my head had not finally won a long and painful battle with my heart. Another bad winter could have brought me down. I had endured too many winters as it was, I knew that.

For a year or so even after I left I thought I might perish anyway, just fade away yearning for Low Birk Hatt and my animals, particularly Rosa, the mother and grandmother of my small herd. My children, I called them. I still cannot bear to go back to visit. It might unbalance things dreadfully.

Anyway, I lifted my head eventually and found that life was still going on, that my old friends were still in place and many more to come. A door opened and I began an entirely new season in my life.

With Her Ladyship, my little white cow, back in the seventies.

It was then that I decided to make up for lost time. I even embarked on a Grand Tour of Europe, which led to my last book and a film series with Barry Cockcroft entitled *Innocent Abroad*, which had very pleasing results.

But I have travelled even more extensively in my own land – the North. Indeed, I have been living like a whirlwind for the last five years, certainly when compared with my previous existence. The invitations have poured into my new home, a very comfortable cottage in a village close to the entrance of dear old Baldersdale. Invitations to go out and about, to see marvellous sights and meet remarkable personalities, all of whom have been so open and friendly.

Sometimes I feel as though I have packed another entire lifetime into my post-Baldersdale period, but then you have to compare that to the fact that I never really went anywhere when I carried the burden of a stock farm in the high Dales single-handed.

And it's been wonderful, more than a person could reasonably hope for. I haven't counted, but I'm sure that I have spent less than half the time in my own bed in the last few years. Indeed, I was only telling a very dear friend recently that I had become a bit like a gypsy just moving on to the next place with no regard to time.

But I would not be able to live permanently in any other place but the Dales. Spending the winter away somewhere warmer is something I could consider – I do hate the snow and the bitterness – but I cannot imagine putting down my roots anywhere else but in my homeland. I would miss the feel of the place, particularly the hills. Anywhere else would mean being an exile.

I well recall my first visit to London when I was forty-eight years old. I had been invited – goodness knows why – to be a guest of honour at the Women of the Year lunch at the Savoy Hotel, and even stayed there in a luxurious riverside suite – but only because another television film was being made about me (by Barry Cockcroft, of course). It was a thrilling occasion, and one I shall never forget. But it was my first experience of a city and I noticed some striking differences. City folk seemed to be a race apart. In the places I'm used to, if you meet a friendly face – and most of them are – you shout out a greeting, even if you have no idea who they are. Crossing the street, going out of or into a shop, anywhere. Everyone does it. It's second nature.

But when I walked around the streets of London – and I do love to visit our capital city because it has much beauty – it really wasn't the same, not by any stretch of the imagination. Everyone seemed to be in such a hurry. And no one seemed to look at the other person passing by. I felt that if I had smiled and bid someone a pleasant 'Good morning', then it might have been misinterpreted and regarded with suspicion.

Now that's a terrible state of affairs!

But do not take that as a criticism of London, or the South, or the people who live down there in the lowlands. Without exception, the people I have met have been most friendly and charming. It's just out in the streets that you see the difference, and I'm sure it's simply an inevitable consequence of city life, with all that rushing about and pressure of business.

In the country, the seasons and not the telephone or the commuter train command our lives. They ordain a much gentler regime really, since you simply have to wait for nature to take its course. There has never been a traffic jam or a points failure in Baldersdale. You may have to work hard in the Dales, particularly in the dark part of the year, but there is always time to take an interest in your fellow man.

So . . . it has been with much pleasure that over recent times I have been able to travel many happy miles without having to leave what I call my own country. It has been a fascinating experience and, with the assistance of my friend of the last twenty years and more, Barry Cockcroft, the basis of this book has emerged.

These are my people and my places. I feel proud to have known them and privileged to be told their stories. I hope and trust you will feel the same.

HANNAH HAUXWELL

A Circumnavigation of the North

*H*annah is back with her own folk. After her romantic fling with foreign parts, touring the more elegant cities and regions of Europe for her *Innocent Abroad* best-selling book and equally successful television series, Miss Hannah returned home with her fledgling appetite for travel honed and ready for more.

In the concluding sequences of both the book and the documentary films, Hannah announced emphatically to several million people that she didn't want that experience to end, and almost immediately on returning to her cottage in Cotherstone arranged a series of excursions and visits which have taken her away from home for weeks on end.

I have known Hannah now for more than twenty years, and for the first eighteen or so I knew exactly where to find her at any given time. She was inexorably chained, physically and emotionally, to Low Birk Hatt and her animals. Then came a fairly long spell when she stayed, with her head down, in Cotherstone – coping with a period of readjustment which had several worrying moments. These days it takes a complex diary system of dates, names and telephone numbers to keep track of her!

Hannah has blossomed in the most remarkable way. I noticed the difference the tour abroad made to her demeanour. She approached the Channel Ferry boat – the first she had ever seen, never mind boarded – full of nerves and apprehension. Six weeks later in Venice she boarded the Orient Express for the trip home with the confidence of a duchess – a very polite duchess, of course. Hannah has the most perfect manners I have ever encountered, and probably holds a world record for the number of times she has said 'thank you' during her lifetime.

She delights in meeting new people and exploring new places. And conversation – how she enjoys talking to people. It satisfies a deep hunger, born of a long, echoing void in her life when she lived alone and in isolation and could go for ten days at a time in winter without meeting another soul. Her only constant companions were a small group of much-cosseted cattle who returned affection in their own way but were not noted conversationalists.

Over the last year or so she has joined with me in a glorious circumnavigation of her North Country, and this book represents the fruits of that journey, a detailed record of what we saw and experienced, and what we were told as Hannah relished the chance of unlimited conversation. All embellished, in the main, by the camera of Mostafa Hammuri, who has worked with me for even longer than I have known Hannah. She has fondly dubbed him 'The Great Mostafa' – the lady does have a way with words.

Several of the people who feature in the following pages have been known to Hannah for many years. She first met some of them at the launches of the film documentaries I have been making for Yorkshire Television since the early 1970s. Legendary personalities in their own right, such as Kit Calvert, Cedric Robinson, Joe Gibson and Dick Chapman. There were many new faces, too, all friendly and all with entrancing, often dramatic tales to tell.

Our progress described a loop, beginning (naturally) in Teesdale and following a line across the top of Swaledale into Stainmore, to Westmorland, the Lake District, Cumbria and Morecambe Bay, Lancashire and back across the Yorkshire Dales almost to Cleveland before concluding in Teesdale.

In essence, it amounts to a tribute . . . a joint affirmation of a total belief that these Northern uplands are as captivating as any in this nation, and the people who live and work there are uniquely possessed of real courage, rich character and endearing personality.

BARRY COCKCROFT

1

High Force . . . and
the Teesdale Roll

I must start with High Force.

It is a place of outstanding beauty – one of nature's masterpieces, you could say – and it is on my doorstep. Indeed, it is one of the few places I actually visited when I was completely unknown by comparison to today, and unable to get out and about much because I was a one-woman farmer with work to do every day of the year.

I have very fond memories of my first trip there, one Saturday after the Second World War when I was in my twenties. I had the chance to go because Uncle Tommy was still alive and able to look after the animals, so I had the luxury of staying with my late cousin, Norman. They took me to Middleton-in-Teesdale carnival, which was a very lively affair with fancy-dress parades and even roundabouts, although I stayed well clear of those!

Next day, I caught the bus to High Force with Lizzie, Norman's wife, and their youngest, Marjorie, who was just a schoolgirl then. We paid a small sum to enter and I was suitably impressed by the sight of all that water crashing down from a height of about sixty feet. We sat down on a log to have a picnic of ham sandwiches.

There was to be an interval of forty years before I was to see High Force again. Some friends of mine from Southport – I have some wonderful new friends these days – took me one summer and, this time, tables and seats had been provided for the picnic, although I imagine the price of admission has risen since my original visit.

I doubt whether Mother or Father ever saw High Force. They never mentioned it. People say I lived a very harsh life until that television programme started to change things, but it was nothing compared to what my parents had to endure.

A visit to 'one of Nature's masterpieces'.

The place has quite a history, as you might expect, and the man who knows as much about it as anyone happens to be a distant relative of mine on the Tallentire side – Mother was a Tallentire. He is Lorne Tallentire, a very clever man with a degree from Oxford. A real local, he only ever left the Teesdale area once and that was to go to Oxford University. Now he earns his living as a professional historian, writing books, doing archaeological research and tracing family trees and old wills. He told me that all the Tallentires in Teesdale are almost certainly descended from a Richard Tallentire who died in 1740 and is

With 'Cousin' Lorne and Anne Tallentire in their garden.

buried in Middleton-in-Teesdale churchyard. He had two wives, one presumably having died, and both our respective families are descended from one or the other. Lorne said the family came originally from the village of Tallentire in Westmorland, which was news to me. They must have liked Teesdale because they clung loyally to the area down the generations. Just a few emigrated to America during the worst depressions, but the rest struggled on.

Lorne has been able to trace the relationship between us by researching the family tree and reckons we are cousins about twenty-five times removed! Anyway, Lorne himself has followed family tradition and stayed true to his roots despite the opportunities that must have opened up for him because of his academic ability. I must say I fully understand because I could not contemplate leaving the hills of Teesdale.

Lorne has written some absorbing books about local places of interest like High Force and, when I was entertained by him and his wife, Anne, who paints lovely pictures, to a traditional Dales tea in their country cottage over the hill from Middleton, I was able to listen to some fascinating stories about the most celebrated spot in Teesdale from a real expert.

High Force is the largest and most spectacular waterfall in Britain. In Hutchinson's history published in 1794 he referred to it as Tees Force. I am inclined to believe the word 'force' comes from the Viking, and we do know the Norsemen colonized this area. It suggests they were impressed by it, but the odd thing is that later in the eighteenth century people generally took quite an opposite view. You see, it was the Age of Reason and wild scenery like High Force was considered unfashionable. Then came the dawn of the Romantic movement around the beginning of the nineteenth century and people went to the other extreme. Travel writers began to use very exaggerated prose when describing High Force. One goes on in vivid style about witnessing a vision of a mountain nymph guiding him to the falls, 'her dress and hair floating to the wind'. Apparently all he saw was a farm girl from Moor Riggs clomping down the side of it. In those days visitors were usually shown to the falls by guides because the paths were so treacherous.

John Wesley visited High Force in 1779 and he expressed some admiration – probably muted by the prevailing atmosphere of the Age of Reason. He certainly didn't like the hills around here, describing them as 'horrid mountains', and noted that it generally seemed to be raining!

Of course, High Force can be a dangerous place for the unwary. I well recall an incident which I was told about when I was a schoolboy. A photographer with a heavy camera and tripod was trying to take a picture of a group at the top of the falls. Instead of asking his subjects to move back to get into the frame, he stepped back himself and went over the edge, taking his camera and tripod with him. I believe that, sadly, he did not survive.

More than twenty years ago a botanist hunting rare plants and wild flowers leaned too far over to get a specimen and plunged in. His body wasn't recovered for several days because it became trapped in one of the deeper parts of the river.

There have been other tragedies further down the valley, some involving the first suspension bridge which was built about 1704 for the lead miners and was considered to be the earliest in Europe. A wedding party came to grief once with fatal consequences and, on another occasion, when one of the chains broke under the weight of a farm group which had Tallentires among them, there was another death. It happened after they had been haymaking at Thomas Tallentire's in Holwick in 1802. They were all merry and had been entertained by the fiddle of Jacob Tallentire, a brother of Thomas – the Tallentires were a musical family. Two fell in the river, and one from the Bainbridge family, having hit a rock, did not resurface. But the other, a Tallentire, lived to tell the tale.

Flash floods used to be a regular menace until Cow Green Reservoir was constructed – in fact, many doubt whether the reservoir really made much of a difference. A huge wall of water would build up following heavy rain higher up the dale and come racing over High Force. They called it the Teesdale Roll.

There was a famous drama in the summer of 1880 when an exceptionally high roll trapped two men in the centre section at the top of the falls. A rescue operation was mounted with ropes being thrown across to the men and one of them was hauled to safety. But the rope snapped when the other poor man, a G.H. Stephenson, was being pulled through the water and he was swept to his death. There have been many other disasters and even more near disasters along the banks of the Tees down the years because it is the second-fastest-flowing river in Britain. Families could be enjoying a day out in the sun unaware that heavy rain was falling higher up the dale and the rock their children was playing on in apparent safety may suddenly be hit by the Teesdale Roll.

Of course, the Tees has occasionally attracted those wishing to take their own lives and there is a famous legend about a girl who is

Cauldron Snout.

reputed to haunt Cauldron Snout, another celebrated set of water-falls about five miles further up the Tees from High Force. The Singing Lady of Cauldron Snout, they call her. It's a beautifully sad story about an innocent young lass who fell in love with one of the miners who stripped out lead from the Pennines during the nineteenth century. There is an old mine shaft in the area. Because some of the miners hailed from villages many miles away from the workings and traditionally went home only once every two weeks, they had to lodge at the mine shop. The swain in question was one of the lodgers, and the girl among the local women who earned money cooking and cleaning for the miners. Apparently, it was a classic case of first love for the girl and for a while the pair were blissfully in love.

But one night he told her that their affair must end, and in her grief and despair she made her way to Cauldron Snout and flung herself into the foaming waters.

It is said that on certain dark nights when the moon appears suddenly from behind a cloud she can be seen from the place where she plunged, shimmering a ghostly white and singing a curiously sad love song. I also understand she has the ability to walk across the water in some of her appearances!

There have been other, rather lighter incidents along the River Tees, some even comic. For instance, before the Second World War when certain Victorian mores were still prevalent, some visitors could not bring themselves to use the word 'snout', because it was just too vulgar. They used to ask locals the way to Cauldron Nose! It even happened to my father.

And then there was the time when some advertising executives decided to use High Force as a background for the publicity material to launch a new model of car. They insisted on a picture of the car right alongside the falls, and they certainly showed remarkable determination. There is only one way to get a car to High Force and that is by suspending it from a helicopter. So they hired one. But there wasn't much room for manoeuvre and I believe the helicopter pilot had a trying time. And they were obliged to construct an artificial rock to perch the car on because nature had not provided anything suitable! But they got their picture in the end. The entire episode must have cost a fortune and certainly astounded the locals.

But even that event was topped as a cause of sheer bewilderment in Teesdale when the film *McKenna's Gold* was shown at the local cinema and later on television. It had Omar Sharif and Gregory Peck hurtling down some river rapids in their pursuit of treasure somewhere ostensibly in the west of America, when there was a sudden cut to a shot of High Force!

I can only assume that the director had a selection of shots of dangerous-looking waterfalls, and considered High Force to be the one best suited to beef up the drama.

I suppose it constitutes a brief moment of international, Hollywood-style glory for our major tourist attraction.

My river – the Tees.

2

Tan Hill . . . and the Pistol-packing Publican

*A*s the curlew flies, Tan Hill is only a few miles over the moors from Teesdale, and it must rank alongside High Force as a place of pilgrimage for those who love the North Country. Tan Hill is a public house and since it is positioned 1,732 feet above sea-level it is the highest in England. It is a truly lonely, isolated place, not far from Stainmore where my mother and father lived for several years – indeed they met and married there.

Tan Hill has no protection from the ferocity of the Pennine winter winds and because of that achieved a kind of national fame in recent years when that very dear farming man, the late Mr Ted Moult, went there to do a television commercial for a certain firm of double-glazing manufacturers. Mr Moult indicated that it was the product's ultimate test.

Way back in the mid thirties it was the licensee of Tan Hill who had celebrity status via the wireless. Mrs Susan Peacock was, I understand, a rather forceful woman who had run the place since 1902 and who stood for no nonsense from awkward customers. It seems she kept a revolver behind the bar for extreme emergencies, and it wasn't one that would fit into a lady's handbag. Like Annie Oakley, Mrs Peacock favoured a man's gun, a Western-style six-shooter. And tradition says that she used it at least once, to frighten off a vagrant who refused to leave the premises and threatened to damage property. One of Mrs Peacock's daughters, who witnessed the incident, has told how the man fled into the night when her mother produced the gun and fired it – but aimed deliberately wide. Apparently, he did return after a decent interval, but never caused trouble again.

Word of Mrs Peacock's strong personality reached the ears of the BBC and she was invited to appear on a very popular radio pro-

With Alec and Margaret Baines, Rollo and Butch (*in the background*). Note the good fire – a daily necessity at Tan Hill!

gramme of the day hosted by a man with the rather curious name of Harry Hopeful, who enjoyed the same kind of public appeal that Wilfred Pickles was to attain in later years. Mrs Peacock made such an impact with her forthright views that she was invited back on the programme on another two occasions, resulting in a lot of publicity in newspapers and magazines. It all led to a considerable increase in people patronizing Tan Hill.

Unfortunately, Mrs Peacock died in 1937 a couple of years after she sprang to prominence. But . . . as you will read a little later on, it may be that Susan Peacock never really left Tan Hill.

It is more than likely that my mother once met Mrs Peacock because she had called at Tan Hill when she was a young single lady. She had an invitation from a friend called Lena Wilson, the daughter of a gamekeeper who lived at Keld, to come and stay and attend an annual supper for either the shepherds or the drivers (the grouse beaters), I'm not sure which. Those occasions were always very important social events in the Yorkshire Dales, and it would have been a rare treat for Mother, who worked very hard keeping house for her Aunt Bessie and a lodger in North Stainmore, playing the organ every Sunday at chapel and earning a little money on the side sewing for a dressmaker. She may have known Daddy at the time, who lived and worked at South Stainmore, but had very little time for courting.

It is a long walk from Stainmore to Keld – but then, folk thought nothing of long treks in those days – and her friend Lena kindly agreed to meet her at Tan Hill and walk back to Keld with her. Because of her Methodist principles I doubt that Mother and Lena had more than a cup of tea and a rest in the pub before going on to the supper. Mother used to tell me it was a glorious meal with an enormous joint of meat. She said the blood followed the knife, so it would not have been to my taste.

Many years ago I called at Tan Hill myself when I was travelling in a van with some neighbours from Baldersdale and we were returning from some sporting event in the Yorkshire Dales. But I only came in for a quick look around because it was such a well-known place. In those days, I was rather wary of public houses. But it is a grand place today even though it stands on its own in the middle of a very desolate stretch of moorland, and it is run by a very interesting couple, Alec and Margaret Baines. Now Mr Baines is a real Dalesman who has bred Swaledale sheep for many years and also farmed cows over at Malham, about forty miles from Tan Hill. But apparently he also managed to work for the local Water Board – quite a few Dalespeople have to supplement their income because stock rearing is no certain way to

Susan Peacock (*right*) the pistol-packing publican herself and friend.

earn a living. Like me, Mr and Mrs Baines are very fond of dogs, and they once owned a cat with a fearsome reputation. The story of how they came to Tan Hill and battled against the elements – not to mention what some believe to be the spirit of Susan Peacock – is fascinating. This is what they told me.

We heard on Yorkshire Television that it was for sale. Never seen the place, neither of us, but I'd watched Ted Moult's double-glazing commercial a few times. Anyway, Margaret agreed to go and look at it and we ended up buying it at auction in 1985. She had worked in a pub before but I had never pulled a pint in my life. The place was in a dreadful state when we took over – I think it would have fallen down if we hadn't arrived to start propping it up. Essentials such as water and electricity services stopped some miles down the hill, so power had to be self-generated and the water was pumped by an old ram pump from a place 400 metres down the moor, which delivered about a pint an hour, and by another contraption run by an old car engine which had to be started up every day. That would fill up a series of about nine tanks in the loft via pipes of all kinds on the ground and joined by jubilee clips, ending with a length of garden hose! Of course, the first bit of frost we had in the November of our first year froze everything solid and we had no water at all. So the decision was made - we had to sink a bore hole.

Margaret Baines tells a highly amusing story of what happened then.

A friend came to look for the water source. He turned up wearing a Crombie coat, jewellery and a hard hat and carrying a twig. Well, I just laughed – I thought he had no chance and told him that we would only pay on results. But off he went around the place with his stick, which eventually started twitching. He pointed to the place and announced that there was definitely water under there. And sure enough there was. Some time later this big drill arrived and went down and down and down – to a depth of 170 feet, and found it! It cost a bit, but it was worth it because the winter of 1985/6 was the worst we have ever had up to now. Our very first winter, and we walked straight into it. But it would have been impossible without water, particularly with the children. We have six girls between us – only two still at home now – and after the initial shock they grew to love this place. The youngest was only two when we arrived. The wind here is a worse problem than the snow. Put your washing on the line here and it will end up in the Irish Sea. I once hung up a sheet with a tiny hole in it and it was ripped to shreds, so I don't dry anything outside now. The wind whips the snow into drifts. There really wasn't a tremendous amount of snow that first winter but we were cut off for six weeks nevertheless. The snow-plough would get through about once a week, but it would fill in again overnight because of the wind. They even had to abandon the snow-plough one night.

Life certainly hasn't been dull since we arrived at Tan Hill. It's just one event after another – you simply don't know what will happen next. About the only certain thing, apart from a white Christmas, is the sheep show on the last Thursday in May. It is the biggest anywhere for the Swaledale breed and the place is totally chaotic. They call it the Royal Show for Swaledale Sheep, and the winners usually

The highest pub in England and its custodians, Alec and Margaret.

go on to make big money at the sales, although there's no selling at the Tan Hill Show – just judging, and very keen it is too. I have to admit that trade has been very good since we arrived. The Pennine Way runs by the place and brings a constant stream of half-dead and dehydrated hikers who fall through the door and sometimes stay for days, pitching their tents on the moor. Once army helicopters landed and the crews came in for a drink. Eventually we decided to keep a diary of all the unusual things that happen here and now we have got five books filled up.

Then there are the strange happenings which may be something to do with Susan Peacock. We built an extension to provide bedrooms for the tourists – Alec did most of it himself – and someone has suggested that maybe Susan doesn't approve. Anyway, things keep happening. The till flies open for no reason, and the beer pumps go down on their own, spilling beer around the place.

People wouldn't believe us at first, but one night I was standing by the fire with Maria, who helps behind the bar. It was snowing like mad outside and there were no customers, when suddenly both beer pumps went down. In front of two witnesses. If it is Susan, she never puts any money in the till! But then, she never takes anything out. Then things keep falling down for no reason. A portrait of a friend of ours, a grand old chap, dropped off the wall inexplicably and I worried all night in case it was an omen. He's still around, I'm glad to say. Mind, he fell off his bike soon after.

Since they came to Tan Hill, Mr and Mrs Baines have owned some of the most wayward domestic animals I had ever heard about. The tale they told me together is both amazing and amusing. My weakness for animals is no secret and I loved meeting those resident at Tan Hill. First and very much foremost was a huge Old English Mastiff bitch weighing over twelve stones called Rollo, which belongs to a lady who works at the pub. Rollo apparently doesn't like Dobermanns – tries to eat them, in fact – and it once took three people to pull her off one poor Dobermann. She's quite friendly with other dogs, however. They also have a nice Jack Russell, like my Timmy. He's called Butch, and he was once a wanderer in the extreme. Then there's a cat called Moledy (as in 'moledy warp' – Dales slang for a waistcoat made from the skin of moles) because its fur is very similar in colour and texture to that of a mole. But it was another cat, no longer living at Tan Hill, which has become something of a legend, as Alec and Margaret explain.

Yes, Speedy was her name. Her story began one weekend just before our first Christmas at Tan Hill when a pregnant cat appeared on our doorstop. I imagine it had been dumped, because it was wearing a really nice collar. Anyway she had three kittens and we kept one – that was Speedy. She was jet black in colour and very slim, with perhaps some Siamese in her. All was normal to begin with and then inexplicably she produced kittens. As far as we knew there wasn't a tom cat for miles around, but we had heard of a wild cat living out on the moor. Farmers say it is very big with only half a tail and tabby in colour. And, sure enough, some of Speedy's kittens have similar markings and colour.

Becoming a mother started all the trouble. Speedy underwent a total change of character and turned vicious, to put it mildly. Not to us, or any other people, but she began to hate dogs and would attack them on sight. It got so bad that the police became involved. A lady came in one day with her two Labradors and Speedy set about them both, driving them under the chairs. It got really nasty. The woman unwisely tried to prise the cat off her dogs and had one of her arms lacerated. So she went to the police and demanded that we should be prosecuted for owning a vicious cat. Apparently, the police couldn't do anything but laugh when they heard the story – not that the lady, understandably, found it at all funny. The policeman told us later that he had gone through all his legal books but could find nothing relating to vicious cats, so nothing could be done about it. Then he said that he wouldn't mind having a kitten off Speedy, since one of his guard dogs had died!

Things went from bad to worse after that. Speedy even took to attacking dogs outside the pub. A couple arrived one day in their car, leaving two Dalmatians in the back while they had a drink. They must have kept a door open because Speedy got in the car and drove the two dogs out. I cannot count how many dogs she has assaulted over the time she was here, but her usual trick was to jump right on to their backs.

There was one memorable occasion when a local hunt was meeting at Tan Hill and man came in with his terrier, which was trained to hunt and kill foxes. He saw Speedy and warned us about his dog, saying it had worried a few cats in his time. Next thing we knew this dog came flying across the pub. Its owner thought it was after Speedy, but he got it the wrong way round. It was Speedy in pursuit of the dog. The man could scarcely believe his eyes and, my goodness, he was upset. Really put out.

Eventually we put signs up everywhere – all around the pub and on a blackboard outside – asking people not to let their dogs out because we had a dangerous cat. Someone even bought us a mat with the inscription, 'This house is protected by an attack cat'. Certainly we never had any problems with mice or rats. In fact, I sometimes wish she was here now because we have some rats out there and Moledy is a bit too young yet to deal with them. Speedy not only kept the local rodent population under control, but she would also bring in gifts of rabbits and even grouse!

She had to go in the end, of course. We were on edge every time a dog came in, so she went to live in Lancaster. A hippie friend of ours who lives in a bus on a farm over there offered to take her, saying she would probably fit in well with the rest of the cats in residence there. We still get news about her because she turns up for her food at the bus and it seems she is still up to her old habits, terrorizing half of Lancaster! We did keep one of her kittens, called Scud, but it vanished mysteriously two days after Speedy left.

We have different problems with Butch, our Jack Russell. He loves to travel and would follow anybody, particularly the Pennine Way walkers. He has been in police custody numerous times, from Keld to Barnard Castle, and the army had him for two days before they brought him back in a military landrover. I fetched him back twice from High Force – and that's thirty miles from here – and once from the youth hostel in Baldersdale. But he seems to have quietened down a bit now and is content with staying at Tan Hill.

Butch's owners seem to have settled in, too. They are obviously well content with Tan Hill themselves, despite the hazards of winter, and continuity is what the place needs. I hear it broke the hearts of several people who tried to make a go of it before them, and Tan Hill suffered because of all the changes of ownership. But Alec and Margaret Baines are Dalesfolk with the stamina and sense of humour necessary to not only survive but prosper at a place like Tan Hill. Alec still keeps a couple of Swaledale sheep himself, thus retaining his links with the land.

They are the true heirs of Susan Peacock and, despite the curious happenings, I am sure she approves of them.

3

Mouthlock Chapel . . . and a Sentimental Journey

*I*f you leave Tan Hill in a westerly direction and head over those rolling moors towards Stainmore for about five miles, you will come across a lonely building which has special significance for me and my family: Mouthlock Primitive Methodist Chapel.

It's a strange situation for a chapel when you think of the sparse population thereabouts and the height of the place – more than a thousand feet above sea-level, which means it has no protection from the ravages of winter. But Mouthlock Chapel was central to the life of my mother all through her childhood and until she was in her late twenties. She was the organist, and deeply involved in all the activities of the chapel – you must remember that chapel life was the social as well as the spiritual centre of every Yorkshire dale. And it was at Mouthlock Chapel in 1920 that Lydia Sayer Tallentire married William Bayles Hauxwell, which led to the birth six years later in Baldersdale of your humble servant, Hannah Bayles Tallentire Hauxwell.

It wasn't easy for Mother to maintain close contact with Mouthlock and all her old friends when she and Daddy moved – reluctantly – ten miles across the moor to Baldersdale. They both loved Stainmore very much and they would have stayed if they had been able. I have always had a fondness for Stainmore itself, considering it to be one of the loveliest places for miles around, bleak, empty, but very beautiful. And there was one occasion which I recall vividly, when Mother made a sentimental journey back. It was during the war when I was about eighteen. She was determined to attend the Sunday School Anniversary at Mouthlock Chapel and spend the weekend with friends. Father was long dead by then, so Uncle Tommy accompanied Mother and me on the first leg of the journey, which had to start on the Friday to make sure we got there. I suppose people these days wouldn't even contemplate walking that far over rough ground carrying personal luggage, unless they were hiking the Pennine Way – but then it was considered normal practice. I had a brand-new tailored coat for the occasion, made by Wilkinsons of Brough (who are still prospering) out of a piece of green material they had left over. Not exactly as good as a velour, but rather that type of material. Anyway, I was quite proud of it.

Mother and I stayed overnight with some friends, Mr and Mrs Buckle, at a farm called Rampson near Brough. Uncle didn't stop – he went to see an old crony of his and then walked back to Low Birk Hatt, arriving in the early hours.

I wanted to see Mouthlock Chapel for the first time very much because Mother had talked so much about it, and I was rather puzzled by its curious location. It really owes its origin to a spot of bother in 1810 when two preachers, Hugh Bourne and William Clowes, fell out with the Wesleyans and were expelled. They carried on preaching in the open air and those that chose to follow them were known as Camp Meeting Methodists and Clowesites. Eventually the two groups got together and became known as Primitive Methodists, joining the breakaway movement which had started in Staffordshire and spread rapidly. A young man from Barnard Castle, Thomas Batty, known as the Apostle of Weardale, set up in Brough on the edge of Stainmore. It was because of his power and influence that the first Mouthlock Chapel was built in 1831 at a cost of £150. A newer and larger building replaced it in 1909, mostly from labour and materials donated freely by its members which kept the expense down to £800. The place thrived for many years, when the congregation was swollen by the railway workers on the new lines being opened and the miners from the pits at Barras and Kettledrums. But the local farmers were the real stalwarts, and they were very pious people. In 1912 the records state that fifty-one adults signed the pledge with the Band of Hope, and that books given as prizes for good attendance at the Sunday School had titles such as *The Life of the Reverend J. Wesley*, *Good Wives and Happy Homes*, and *No Gains Without Pains*!

It was certainly a busy and happy place the weekend Mother and I attended. We went to all the services and had tea with a Mr and Mrs Alderson who Mother knew well from the old days. The fact that my mother was in the congregation was mentioned by the chairman, Mr Arthur Bird, a nice welcome which pleased her very much. We set back for Baldersdale on either the Monday or the Tuesday, I forget which now. But I do recall it poured down so badly that we couldn't see

Mother and me, when I was a teenager.

properly and had difficulty following the track over the moor. My new coat got soaking wet and I was very worried about it, but it survived. Indeed, it's not long since I parted with it.

In recent times I have met a grand old man called Henry Dixon, who has turned eighty-eight but retains very clear memories of my mother and father when they lived in Stainmore. He and his wife, Mary, celebrated their Diamond Wedding in 1992 and received a message from the Queen. As you might imagine, I listened with keen interest to tales of Henry's childhood when he was a regular attender at Mouthlock Sunday School, and his memories of my parents.

All our family, including my mother and father, were brought up at Upmanhow, which is close to Mouthlock Chapel. I well recall Willie Hauxwell, Hannah's father, walking over from North to South Stainmore to work a piece of land his uncle had taken over alongside where Hannah's mother lived. In winter, after he had finished toiling, he was obliged to sleep the night in the hay. When I was five

Isolated, and a thousand feet above sea level – Mouthlock Chapel.

I moved to North Stainmore but had to go to school at South Stainmore, so many's the time I've walked back home with Willie Hauxwell. I don't think there could have been a better worker on the face of the earth than that man. Put a rake in his hand and he would go at it like a race-horse! I knew Lydia, because she was such a leading light at the chapel, but I don't know much about their courtship and marriage because by that time I'd had to leave the area to find work. I went into service at a farm in Kirkby Stephen. Boys had to grow up fast in those days. I remember a time just after the First World War started when my father was ordered to grow potatoes to help the war effort. One night he told me to rise early the next morning to take muck to the potato patch before I went to school, so I did, harnessing our little black Galloway horse to a cart and setting about it. I led and tipped two loads, went home for my breakfast, and then walked three miles to school. I was ten years old at the time.

To encourage us farm lads to go to school, the lady at the big house, Mrs Abercrombie, who came from monied folks, used to give us half a crown if we didn't miss a day's schooling during the year. She would dock sixpence for every day we missed. I only got two shillings one year because I had to take a day to go to the Mouthlock Chapel Band of Hope Demonstration Day. I wouldn't have

With Henry Dixon at the chapel entrance.

Top Henry Dixon about to open the door.

Above Mr and Mrs Dixon and their letter from the Queen.

A poignant moment – was this the organ my
mother once played?

missed that for anything. We marched around with banners, and then had a slap-up tea, races with prizes and free rides on a round-about. I know I went with three halfpennies in my pocket, and brought a halfpenny back!

Mouthlock Chapel used to give us a good Christmas party with plenty of fruit cake, but no presents as I recall. But I have a very plain memory of the day the new Mouthlock Chapel opened in 1909 and I attended the ceremony. I was only five at the time, and the reason I recall it so well is because there was a dickens of a storm. Thunder and lightning, everything. It seemed to me at the time that Heaven wasn't too pleased about the event!

Sadly, Mouthlock Chapel was closed down in the summer of 1991. The railway lines had closed, the pits had finished and young men were leaving the farms to seek their fortune in foreign places. The chapel was obviously suffering a drop in interest back in the late forties, when the records reveal that a new boiler was added to the heating system at a cost of £27 – a very necessary item during the winter, I imagine. Someone wrote a wry little note in the Trustees' Records: 'The chapel is now lovely and warm. It is a pity so few people come to worship.'

I paid another very sentimental visit recently, and was very moved by what I saw. The chapel has been sold, fortunately to a religious organization, and all the pews have been taken out. So has the pulpit, reputed to be the finest on the local circuit, a beautiful thing magnificently hand carved out of pitched pine. The man who carved it was called Tom Lee, who lived a fair distance away. It seemed that he spent so much time and effort completing the pulpit that he had the opportunity to meet, court and marry a local girl. I found that the organ remained, marooned in a sea of dust and bits of masonry. It looked so forlorn. I tried the keys, the very keys my own mother may have played for so many years, but there was no sound.

I am not ashamed to admit I was close to tears at this point. All the memories came flooding back. It was such a special place for my parents. They had spent their young lives contentedly in Stainmore.

When they were obliged to move to Baldersdale to share a home filled with ageing and ill relatives, I know they weren't really happy any more. I mean no disrespect to anyone, but it isn't easy, then or now, for different generations to live in rather cramped conditions under the same roof. On top of that they had the extra burden of a baby and a terrible depression to cope with. I know they often thought about those days in Stainmore. I remember Mother once saying, and Daddy agreeing, that they had no peace, had no home when they left.

4

Appleby Fair

*T*he road that skirts the perimeter of Stainmore is the A66, a frighteningly busy road filled with the roar of juggernauts, racing to and from the M6 motorway. It is an incongruous sight, really, with the turmoil of that road contrasting so starkly with the silent sweep of the fields and hills of Stainmore, a vast patchwork quilt of heather, dry stone walls, hay meadows and rough moorland, where there are more rabbits on the narrow little roads than vehicles.

But during the early part of June, just for a few days, there is a pronounced unevenness in the flow of traffic when a particular type of conveyance, an echo of more leisured times, joins the A66 and creates chaos. It means the Romanies are on the move!

Appleby Fair is the great, tumultuous, annual celebration of a way of life that goes back so far in time that there are no positive records. They came out of the East, or so it is believed, alert, eager, swarthy men with no roots who moved on continually from one place to the next. And always with horses. So every June thousands of the Travelling Folk converge on Appleby, in Westmorland, with their wonderful coloured horses – piebalds, skewbalds, every colour a horse can be – and their wagons. A lot have vardoes, those romantic, bow-roofed caravans, which haven't changed in design for centuries. Some are lavished with gilt carvings and painted scenes, and all shine with care and pride. And behind each one you will see a wagon with dogs perched on top, drawn by horses.

I do admire the nonchalance with which they mingle with the articulated lorries, vans and cars, most driven by people who are clearly agitated at having to move at the pace of a horse until there is a chance to overtake. The gypsies – that's the generic term for these devil-may-care people, I understand – seem to be totally oblivious to the confusion and irritation that surrounds them on all sides. I suppose it is a

statement – of defiance, of freedom perhaps. I understand that some Romanies do not exist as far as the state is concerned. They have no National Insurance number, they don't register births and they run their own lives in their own way. Now that *is* freedom, although I imagine it can lead to certain difficulties.

Anyway, along the A66 they trot, turning off for Appleby, much to the relief of the other road users for whom life is one long dash. Not that life is that tranquil when the gypsies arrive at the fair. Quite the opposite. But it is a totally enjoyable level of high activity. The whole place is a theatre with action, a bit of drama now and then, and a wealth of character.

I did go to Appleby Fair when I was a teenager in 1947 and it was a memorable experience. John and Marie Thwaites took Uncle Tommy and me in their car. They lived at High Birk Hatt, just up the fields from our farm, but it was to be their last year in Baldersdale. John's father, old John, had died just before the big storm in 1947. Young John had managed to afford a car, which was unusual in our day, and he was very generous with giving lifts to neighbours. I recall the day well as one of the more exciting ones of my youth. I have mental images of lots of horses running about, some pulling carts and others ridden bare-back, and one had to be nimble to avoid being knocked over. Lots of noise, movement and strong men slapping each other hard on the hand as they concluded deals. Obviously, horses are fundamental to the lives of the gypsies, and a lot of trading took place. And they had such control over them – clearly, they are brought up with horses from childhood.

For years I nursed an ambition to go back to Appleby Fair. In 1992 the opportunity arrived. It was a beautiful day, hot and clear, and I was taken first to watch the horses being washed in the river. It's obviously a ritual, with lots of posing and dramatics as the owners, stripped to the waist, ride them into the deeper places. Then they are rinsed down again before being taken up the hill for the trading. Large crowds of tourists gather on the bridge and the banks of the river, clicking away with their cameras. I became a touch concerned with the way they urged the horses out of their depth, and some were tied to the tail of the horse in front. I don't think some of them liked it overmuch, but they were all so obedient and swam safely to the bank. I'm afraid I became a bit of a tourist attraction myself, because dozens of people recognized me and went up to shake hands, take my picture and obtain my autograph. One Romany came up with a £5 note to sign, and that started a real fashion. I cannot imagine the total value of the notes I signed or what exactly they proposed to do with them. It would seem

Washing the horses in the river at Appleby Fair.

such a waste to stick them in an autograph album. I met and talked to some fascinating people, including some genuine Romanies. One was a Mr Chambers Lee – the Lees are one of the classic Romany families – and he had a horse and a superbly decorated flat cart. He had a variety of tattoos on his arms, one commemorating his great grand-father, Randle Lee, who was apparently a very famous prize-fighter. He said he came every year without fail to Appleby, travelling 300 miles from Essex. But his wife had been unable to come this year and he was having to return early because of a major problem with one of his best mares. He said the mare was suffering from laminitis because it had been the hottest May for the last 130 years, would you believe.

This had brought on the laminitis which causes stiffness in the legs around the hock, causing so much pain it was difficult for the horse to move. Mr Lee was obviously very worried about his mare, which he had bred himself, and said the only way to cure it was to starve her for four or five days. Being cruel to be kind, he put it.

I know from personal experience just how attached you can get to horses, and they all have different personalities. We had several at Low Birk Hatt down the years. There was Snip the mare, who was a bit frisky and gave me a few problems when I was using her to sweep the hay, probably because she sensed I had no confidence. I ended up with a sprained wrist one haytiming. She would take a nip at you as well, if you didn't watch out. But Dick the horse was a nice little chap, and much better mannered. Then we had Prince and Blossom and a few foals. Uncle was very good with horses and I heard that my father was, too. They say Father could jump straight off the ground and mount

The autograph queue (*above*).

Conversation with a travelling man, and a photo opportunity (*opposite*).

40

Scenes from a fascinating
day at Appleby Fair.

and ride a horse bareback. Although he wasn't very big, he also had a talent for breaking and training horses.

I can feel for that man worrying about his mare because we had a tragedy with a foal once. It was a lovely filly, a bay-and-white skewbald which was born in the spring of 1947, and had such long legs that I called her Daddy Long Legs. During August, the horses had been left further down Baldersdale, at a place called Hury, to start with haytiming, and one morning I set off on my own to tend them. And I found Daddy Long Legs lying dead. There was no sign of injury, but there had been a violent thunderstorm during the night so she may have died of fright. Oh dear, I was so upset because I was very proud of her. I did cry.

It is very rare these days to find a working horse on a farm, so I suppose we can thank the gypsies for keeping the tradition alive. They really are colourful people with such character on their faces, which are without exception tanned from their outdoor life. I must say I prefer that type. I mean no offence to fair, Nordic fellows, but I think a good-looking, dark-haired man is always more striking. As long as they have a nice personality to go with their looks, of course. They remind me of the song about the maid who ran off with the raggle-taggle gypsy.

Mind, I've always been a touch wary about gypsies. They came into Baldersdale from time to time and we always bought something like pegs or ribbons, or gave them a cup of tea, because we didn't want to incur their wrath. No gypsy curses, thank you!

And I do like their kind of coloured horses. I prefer them to the thoroughbred kind which may have lovely long legs, for such fine bones can easily be broken. And we all know what happens to a horse with a broken leg. There were scores of bonny piebalds and skewbalds being put through their paces on the hill above Appleby, which becomes a small town during the fair, with streets of caravans, some very ornate, and lots of stalls selling everything for horses. There were some splendidly decorated carts on offer as well.

And what skilful riders those gypsies are. Young or old, they almost seem to form part of the horse, particularly when moving at speed, and most were capable of riding bareback without a bridle, and still controlling the horse without apparent effort. I don't think that my father would have been able to do that, good as he was.

Personally, I never took to horse riding in spite of every opportunity down the years. We did possess a saddle, too! In fact, I've never ridden a horse. I stopped working with them at Low Birk Hatt after I had been on my own for about three years. The last one was Thomas, who had a lovable temperament but was as fat as butter because he

Meeting Mr Randle Lee, from an old Romany family.

didn't eat to live, he lived to eat. Horses can be so affectionate and you grow attached to them, but disaster always seems to be just around the corner with them.

I have had several unfortunate experiences.

First, there was the shock of finding the foal. Later on, Blossom, a nice miniature Clydesdale with feathers on her feet, developed a heart condition and had to go. Then, to cap it all, my Thomas went lame. A good neighbour who was very knowledgeable came to give his opinion, and said that it was so serious that sooner or later he would go down and not be able to get up again. He very kindly agreed to take him away, to spare me some of the pain.

But it was a horrid and a heart-breaking business and I could never bring myself to have a horse at Low Birk Hatt from then on.

5

Ullswater and Donald Campbell
. . . a Place for Heroes

A reminder of home – the trees and tranquil waters of Ullswater.

*U*ntil I began what I call my second life, the Lake District was just a place I had heard and read about. With the sole exception of a Sunday School day trip to Keswick before the Second World War, now just a dim memory, my personal experience was nil. And yet, if you glance at a map, the lakes and the Yorkshire Dales are joined at the hip, so to speak, like Siamese twins. All part of a corridor, running east to west – or the other way round if you prefer – across the far North of England. Where one ends, the other begins, and the boundary is marked by the M6 motorway.

Since I retired from farming in the winter of 1988 I have travelled more than in the first sixty years of my life, and the Lake District has figured quite strongly. One particular corner has become quite dear to me and that's Glenridding, near the end of the west side of Ullswater. I have a particular weakness for a mix of water and trees because they remind me of my old home in Baldersdale, perched on the side of a reservoir and close by a little wood. And Glenridding has an abundance of both, of course, as well as being such a tranquil place. I found it through the kindness of the owners of the Ullswater Hotel, Mr and Mrs Hutchinson, and their daughter Beverley, who manages this very large and elegant hotel. I've stayed there a couple of times, and after I'd settled in I noticed there were several photographs around of Donald Campbell, that rather dashing young man who broke world speed records for Britain. Obviously he had some connection with the place, which surprised me because I had always associated him with Coniston Water, where he died so tragically trying to set a new water-speed record. But it was his own record he was chasing and he

actually set the original one on Ullswater and, it would seem, spent a lot of time in the Glenridding area. I rather think Donald Campbell lived for a while in the shadow of his equally famous father, Sir Malcolm Campbell, who blazed a very spectacular trail himself in his bid to become the world's fastest man. But his son certainly emerged from the shadows in the end and became a truly heroic figure, a real swashbuckler in the great British tradition set by Drake and Raleigh. Braving extreme danger for the glory of his nation's flag.

I made some enquiries and found that Donald Campbell had become a most popular figure with several of the locals, who got to know him very well. I even met a group of them in the hotel and they told me stories which were so interesting, and they even cast a new light on this truly courageous and unique man.

The heroic Donald
Campbell and Bluebird.

Listening to the stories of Lakeland men – Harold Iredale (*top left*), Eddie Pool (*top right*), Walter Burnett (*bottom left*) and George Wilson (*bottom right*).

They were all true Lakelanders, with typical weatherbeaten, countrymen's faces and they had some remarkable personal backgrounds themselves. The one who seemed to know Donald Campbell best was a man whose family had made a living on and around Ullswater since the time of Elizabeth I. But Eddie Pool, just turned sixty, said his family name was originally Pols, and they were miners brought from Germany by Lord Burleigh, on the direct orders of Queen Bess. Her sea captains – who knows, maybe even Drake among them – had discovered that if the bottom of a ship was copper plated it resisted crustacea, algae and seaweed, and they set a pace that could outmanoeuvre the Spanish ships. Perhaps Drake's defeat of the Armada may have been partially due to our copper-bottomed boats. Apparently, the Spanish were not aware of this method themselves. Burleigh knew that copper could be found in the fells of Lakeland, but he had no miners skilled enough to dig it out. Germany had, so a fair number of them were persuaded to come over. Therefore, some Lakeland families were originally German and their names were Anglicized down the generations. For instance the Brauns became Browns, the Thyssens became Tysons and so on.

Eddie's late father, Johnny Pool, was, it seems, Donald Campbell's closest confidant among the locals. Apparently, Donald was fascinated by his tale of his experiences fighting the Germans in the First World War – but the man never knew he was of German extraction himself. This is what his son told me.

Yes, my father saw a lot of action at the front, even fought at the Somme. He enlisted in the Borderers, became a machine-gunner at first and then transferred to the tank corps when tanks were introduced into warfare for the first time. He and Donald Campbell spent hours talking about tanks and guns, going into minute technical detail about the merits of this and that engine and various calibres of gun. Now, my old feller hated the Germans as a result of the war, but never knew anything about the family's German connection. I would have given a lot to see his face had he ever found out.

He had a deep knowledge of mechanical things, a passion he shared with Campbell, although his father, grandfather, and who knows how many previous generations, had worked in the mines bringing out lead when the copper ran out. His mother, my grandmother, refused to allow him to follow tradition, saying she didn't want him to be dead at forty through silicosis like so many others. They were treated terribly, those old miners. They were called tramp miners because they had to go from place to place looking for work, and sometimes there were riots over conditions and pay. I heard tell of one occasion when the militia had to be called out in Keswick and the miners were driven on to an island on Derwent Water.

Anyway, Dad became the local coalman and haulage contractor. Donald Campbell had to pass by our house to get to the boathouse and slipway where they kept *Bluebird*, and he often called. In fact, I think he used to hide away from people trying to pester him, particularly the press.

He had a bad time with the reporters. I suppose he was always being compared with his father, Sir Malcolm, who was a world-beater in his time. Donald had tried and failed more than once for a land-speed record, and I think the newspaper men wouldn't let him forget it. I went to one press conference with him and they were abusive straight away, saying that nothing was happening and wanting him to go out and do something there and then. One reporter said it was costing his paper a lot of money keeping him there, so Donald said that could easily be solved – why didn't he get on a bus and go home!

He and his team were here for months around 1954 and my dad and I got to know them all. Sometimes we would go night fishing for trout and come back at one in the morning to find Leo Villa, the famous mechanic, and the Norris brothers working on the boat in the building specially constructed for the job, and we'd have a chat.

Donald was a tremendous engineer. Everything involving engineering came easy to him, and I think if he had chanelled his ambition towards that instead of racing he could have been immensely successful. I know Leo Villa thought that too, and he should have known. I was told Donald's father didn't know the back end of a machine from the front. He would wait until the engineers had finished, then climb in and drive it to its limits. But the son wanted to understand everything, and did.

Donald was a good man and a brave man, never boastful. He even used to drive his Jaguar sports car around the place at a respectable speed when you'd expect a man like him to drive very fast. Some of the locals thought he could be a bit aloof, and maybe he was at times. But that was undoubtedly due to the strange life he led, not knowing from one day to the next whether he would get killed out there. Mostly he was very happy to chat to locals in the street. In fact, I can tell you a story which illustrates just how thoughtful he could be. There was a young lass – still living around

Strolling round Ullswater.

here, by the way – who would run errands for Donald and his crew, fetching cigarettes and ice creams, things like that. Anyway, she hadn't turned up for a time and Donald saw her in the street and asked why. She told him that one of the men Lord Wakefield, the owner of the land on which the boathouse was built, had sent down to keep an eye on things had told her to stay away. He promptly told her that she could pop down to the boathouse any time she wished and that the man in question would be told in no uncertain terms to mind his own business. I admired him for that.

Donald made himself even more popular with the community when he donated a cup to be presented annually to the local sports-man or sportswoman of the year. It was one his father had won in a hill climb years ago and it's still awarded to this day, a permanent memorial to him.

He certainly brought crowds to Ullswater. There's never been so many people coming here before or since, with crowds and cars filling every available space, all striving for a glimpse of *Bluebird* on the water. And he was out there a lot doing trials. *Bluebird* looked like a tin can in the water and I thought there was no way he would set a new record when I first saw it, but once it got going and lifted out of the water it was a different thing altogether.

As a matter of fact, Father and I knew he was going to break the record the Thursday evening before the Saturday he officially did it. He took *Bluebird* out for a trial and I'm sure it was the fastest he ever did. We watched as he went down the lake at a hell of a rate of knots, and came back even faster. When he climbed out on the slip-way, he walked up to my father, winked and said he thought he had done over sixty miles an hour! He was obviously very pleased with himself. I would have put it nearer 240 miles per hour, but there was no one there to record it. Then he said he would go for the record on the Saturday.

Listening with me to Eddie was another local who knew the man himself. George Wilson is a farmer and a magistrate and he was in a privileged position when Donald Campbell launched *Bluebird* that Saturday.

He had his telemeter van in one of our fields, which had all the equipment to monitor the stresses and strains of the boat, and to record everything Donald Campbell and Leo Villa said. That morning the conditions were right, the timekeepers were in position, but oddly enough very few people were present because it was early. Even the press were mostly missing. We sat outside the van with the job of keeping all the press away because everything said between Donald and Leo was copyright. But the engineers were good enough to turn up the sound so we could hear. My memory was of the excitement in Donald's voice on the first run. But he broke his aerial doing it and there was no transmission on the way back. The noise *Bluebird* made when he opened her out was remarkable. It echoed round and round the valley as though it couldn't get out. Strangely, it wasn't an offensive noise, though a jet plane was nothing by comparison.

He knew he had broken the record on the way down, but it has to be based on the mean of two runs over the measured mile, so he didn't know for a while if he had really done it. When it was finally confirmed that he had – by pushing it just over 200 miles an hour – there was more a sense of relief than jubilation.

I found him to be an open and friendly man. We lived next door to the cottage his mother, Lady Campbell, had rented and she was a

Alongside an example of the skill of the Lakeland wallers.

most charming lady. I recall an hilarious incident when she once rang my mother when she was having problems with her Triplex grate, which was a kind of forerunner of the Rayburn and the Aga. Mother was trying to explain by going through all the motions with her hands, forgetting that Lady Campbell couldn't see her!

Of course, he left Ullswater for Coniston where he died trying to break his own record. It was an understandable decision because the margin for error on Ullswater was very limiting. Ullswater isn't straight, you see – it has three legs and the speeds he was achieving meant that if he pushed it any further there was a chance he wouldn't be able to pull up in time.

Eddie Pool remembers two incidents which came close to ending in tragedy because of the hazards presented by Ullswater.

He very nearly hit an island once. Leo told him on the radio to be more careful because he had just missed it and Donald said: 'What bloody island, I never saw an island!' I believe they had to modify the boat after that to try to reduce the spray. On another occasion he almost ended up amongst the Jubilee Seats – old iron chairs put there on the bank to mark Queen Victoria's Jubilee. He came to a halt a few feet away, and Leo went mad.

On the day of the record I was just dropping off a load of coal when I saw him go down to the boat, so I pulled the wagon in to watch. My father and brother were haymaking at the time – we had sheep and cattle to feed – and they stopped to see it as well. We all carried on working afterwards, but the word that he had succeeded at last soon went round. I think Donald even came to tell Father himself.

There was a party to celebrate, but for some reason it was held somewhere at the other end of the lake, and not in our village. There was a certain degree of unhappiness about this but there was probably a practical reason. A bit of a farewell do was organized for Donald when he was packing up to leave, but it was a bit low-key.

It was inevitable he wouldn't come back to Ullswater because of the problems and I recall he went to Australia and America to attempt records before he returned to Coniston Water and the final tragic chapter.

I don't know what happened because his team were obviously so careful that I did think for a time that there would never be any silly accidents. But, traditionally, these fellows die, don't they? Seagrave did, and several others trying to break speed records. Donald Campbell once said to us that he saw no reason why a boat shouldn't go at well over 300 miles per hour. Maybe he expected to do it, and took one risk too many.

Those pictures on television of *Bluebird* looping the loop on Coniston will always stick in the memory. Father was devastated. He cried like a baby.

As I listened to these hardy men of the Lakeland fells it turned out that Donald Campbell wasn't the only hero around Ullswater. The conversation, as we sat overlooking that beautiful stretch of water, veered round to the basic reason many of their ancestors had arrived in the first place – mining. And I heard a story which was terrible and yet vividly demonstrated extreme bravery on the part of two of the men I was with. It happened in the early fifties when there was a disaster at Greenside, the local lead mine. It was one of the biggest in the country, apparently the first in the world to be electrified, and during its heyday employed well over three hundred people, including Eddie Pool, who was a fitter, and another of our group, Walter Burnett, who was an electrician. Eddie told the story.

It all began for me at nine in the morning precisely. My boss told me and my mate to get to the mine mouth as fast as we could because something had gone wrong. When we got there we met two miners, one stumbling around with a bleeding head and the other unconscious. We didn't know it at the time, but there had been a fire in a wood-lined shaft. Anyway, I reckoned that if they could get out we could get in so we set off inside. We met another miner who was staggering like a drunkard. My mate looked after him and I went on alone. Then I came across a group of miners, who were acting very strangely. I didn't realize it then but they were suffering the effects of carbon monoxide gas, which can affect men like too much beer. Some were laughing, some were crying and others were wanting to fight. When I got to the pit shaft top there was me and an Irish lad called Danny Wilson, who was as strong as an ox. Then my pal, Johnny Miller, arrived and the three of us set off down in the cage. We got to the start of the next shaft which was 175 fathoms deep and found a lot more half-conscious miners, including Jack Hamilton,

The mouth of Greenside mine, circa 1950.

the foreman, who was in a hell of a state. Well, we were concerned about the rest – where were they? Down another stage obviously. As preparations were made to go further down, a miner called George Gibson grabbed my lamp because he had forgotten his. I protested that I couldn't work without light but he vanished off down the rope-ladders. Johnny thrust his own lamp in my hand and followed George. I went to the hoist and eventually heard them signal to bring the cage up. But it wouldn't work. As it turned out, a pipe had broken and the compressor wasn't operating. So I ran back towards the bottom of the shaft and I fell for no reason. I was also going through very cold water but couldn't feel anything. The carbon monoxide was getting to me. But I was twenty years old then, just out of the army and as fit as I've ever been, and I had enough brains left in my head to realize what was happening. So I went back and got on the telephone to tell people at the top to send down oxygen bottles. But nothing happened . . . nobody came. So I went back to the shaft and started going down the ladders but that horrible stuff was coming up to meet me. I couldn't breathe, so I knew it was useless to go on and climbed back to the hoist. In desperation I grabbed the wire rope and tried to pull the cage up. It was stupid – Lord alone knows what it weighed and it was on a 73-degree slope. But I was desperate . . . I wanted to save Johnny Miller, my mate. He was the one on my mind because he was a great character and an ex-marine commando.

Then I passed out. But I was the luckiest man alive because Walter here arrived with a few other electricians to try and get some of the people out. And they found me. They knew what the problem was by then but they still took the risk to try a rescue bid. Trouble was we didn't really understand gas – it had never happened before. There was no danger in a lead mine apart from the dust, which began to affect you at forty and killed you at fifty. Apart from rushes of rock or accidentally blowing yourself to bits with explosives, that was the only hazard.

There was nothing Walter and his mates could do for the men at the bottom of the mine. There were four of them. George Gibson and Johnny Miller had gone down to try and save a man called Leo O'Leary. And, unknown to us, another miner called Dick Mallinson had also gone down to try and get to Leo. He had managed to lift him into a kibble, a big bucket which came up on an air-line, but then the gas got him before he could start to try and make it work.

I was the only survivor of that group.

The lads who died trying to save lives got the Edward Medal, the

Another glimpse of the glories of Ullswater.

highest award a miner can get. Walter received the BEM and I had a letter from the Queen.

Nobody knows how the fire started and it's a miracle that sixty more didn't perish. One man nearly lost his foot – in fact I thought it was sure to be at the bottom of the pit. He was coming up in a cage when he collapsed and one of his legs poked out. When I saw him there was just a bundle of blood instead of a foot.

Now I had a day off after the disaster – just one, mind – and when I came back to work I met this lad's father. He was in a terrible state, said they had set his son's leg and could I take him to see him. I told him I would, but then said I had a disappointment for him because his foot had been taken clean off – I'd seen it. He insisted he had been told differently so I told him not to believe it. When we arrived the doctor confirmed it was true. I was amazed. Apparently the man, by some reaction or other, had pulled his foot, hanging by sinews, up his trouser leg behind his calf. So it was hidden from me when I saw him. How they put it together again I will never know.

They closed Greenside mine in 1961 but it still gave employment to the locals because the Atomic Energy Authority took it over. The Russians and the West had negotiated a ban on testing atomic weapons and our side wanted to try an experiment. They decided to place a large amount of TNT in Greenside, set it off and record the shock wave around the world. All the way to Australia, and back. That way they would have scientific knowledge to find out if the Russians were breaking the agreement by testing atomic weapons in some far-off place, such as Siberia. There was plenty of work for our chaps, cleaning the place out and cementing the levels. They had vehicles all around the shaft and I found work servicing them.

Trouble was, after the explosion two more miners died. From carbon monoxide poisoning, would you believe? After the dust had settled, one of the ex-miners went in to show a Spanish chap, who had never been in a mine before, where he used to work. The TNT had created the same effect as the fire which had caused the disaster, and they walked right into it.

6

Where Have all the Otters Gone?

*I*t was an inspiring time for me, the days I spent on the shores of Ullswater, admiring the beauty of the place itself and listening to those absorbing stories told by very special men. But before I left, Eddie Pool told me a sad story which I am afraid is symptomatic of what is happening around the world. Eddie may be a mechanical man by trade, but at heart he is a true countryman. I suspect he was always happiest out on Ullswater on his boat, rod and line in hand, or tramping the fells with his dogs. As you know, I am fond of all canines and Eddie had four when I met him, Lakeland terriers bred from the Bedlington variety which he believes were originally brought to this country by the German miners and named after the pit village of Bedlington in Northumberland, where they worked. They are used for hunting fox and rabbit. Since boyhood Eddie has had daily contact with a wide variety of wildlife, particularly otters, which are really magnificent creatures, as well as herons, sandpipers, dippers and water rats. But not any longer. He says they have all disappeared, and even the fish have gone from the lake.

Aye, I recall the time when on an all-day fishing trip using flies, I could land fifty trout, no trouble at all. At one time I even contemplated giving up my job at the mine and becoming a full-time fisherman, but since the trout season doesn't last very long I thought better of it. Fly fishing from a boat is an art in itself. Quite apart from casting the fly properly, working the boat is just as important. Dad and me would go out in a row boat, and drift with the wind, using the oars to keep us crossways. We used to be out there every night, nearly. Big fish were rare in Ullswater – the record catch I knew about was 4 lbs – but they were really tasty and very good fighters. Small maybe, but you certainly knew about it if you hooked one from three-quarters of a pound upwards.

I've still got a boat but now it is used once a fortnight, if that. They're just gone, simple as that. You'd be lucky to land three or four these days. The odd trout is getting back into the streams leading into Ullswater, but years ago if you walked up the river between Ullswater and Brotherswater you would have seen a thousand trout, just swimming about. Look over any bridge and there they were. You can do the same walk today and be lucky to spot one.

And then there were the otters. They really fascinated me. Any summer's night once you could go down to that lake and see a dozen otters. And if the moon was out and the lake flat calm you could see the waters parting as they swam along. If you were out fishing at night they were round the boat, smelling the fish, and if you left any on the shore they would go and pinch them.

An otter and its supper.

I used to spend hours watching them, particularly at dusk when they were feeding. They were just like dogs under the water, scratching around heaps of stones looking for eels and fish hiding away. Beautiful creatures they were, really tremendous. The dogs used to go for them, of course, and if they came across any on the shore there would be a hell of a fight until the otter got back in the water. There could be a bit of sport with water rats too, when the dog found them under the roots of the alder trees which stick out like big fingers. But they're all gone now, too – otters, fish and water rats. Strange thing – it seemed to happen overnight. They just vanished. I can even pin it down to the night. I had a pup called Tony, and that night he rushed into a hole and met an adult otter which knocked him so hard he flew backwards into the lake. I thought, that'll teach you something, Tony! Now that was the very last time I ever saw an otter on Ullswater. Tony died ten years ago and he was fourteen, so that adds up to around 25 years. The trout and the water rats vanished at the same time, and the dippers and sandpipers.

How could it happen so quickly and to so many species? It's worried me ever since it happened. It was too sudden for the normal kind of pollution. There was pollution from the mine, I suppose, but that stopped long before. Some say it could have been the stuff they used for sheep dipping, which was DDT based and banned now, others point to that time when the nuclear power station just up the coast from here they used to call Windscale, blew its top and spewed out radioactive material over thirty years ago. Then there's the business of acid rain. I read somewhere that an expert said it was particularly lethal in the Lake District because it diluted the aluminium in the soil and washed it down to the lakes, poisoning the fish. Someone's bound to know, or at least have a good idea, someone in the government. But they aren't telling us. I wonder why they don't do something about bringing the otter back to Ullswater, and if they up and go again they might be able to work out the reason. It's strange, anyway, that the otter hasn't come back on its own initiative, because they are supposed to be a travelling animal.

Some people have suggested that the mink may have had something to do with it, but the otters and the fish had gone long before they came on the scene. Now minks can be deadly things, and the first generation which escaped from the farms were really bad little creatures which worried everything that they came across. I don't think they knew what they were doing, just totally confused. But

they were succeeded by generations bred in the wild and they are not so bad. Mind, I've noticed that they've quickened up a lot – they can move like lightning. And nothing preys on them either, except humans perhaps.

Another point that puzzles me is that whatever happened to drive away the otters, fish, water rats, dippers and sandpipers didn't affect other species. Crows, mallard, ducks, seagulls, herons and

Foraging among the rocks.

64

squirrels have multiplied around Ullswater. Bad winters sometimes knock back the squirrel and the heron but they always come back.

I was told that the carrion crow is generally hated by countrymen, particularly shepherds, because it is an extremely cruel bird. Harold Iredale, forty years a shepherd and still working as he approaches eighty, has some horrifying tales to tell about this bird.

Yes, it's the worst there is. You can spot the difference between an ordinary crow and this one, because it's rather larger and it has a big black beak with a bit of whisker on either side. And the things it does to sheep, particularly lambs, is disgusting. I've heard of foxes and even badgers and otters worrying sheep but I have never seen it happen. I have often seen carrion crows setting about new-born lambs, driving their beaks into their navels and breaking open their innards. I once watched one land on the head of a distressed ewe, lean over and peck out an eye and eat it. And the poor sheep was still very much alive. The owner came running up and told me that damned bird had done the same thing four times in that very field and he was going to shoot it.

But they are not easy to pot. Too damned clever. You might get one, but after that they're up and away, even if you produce a walking-stick. I hate carrion crows so much that I cannot find words bad enough to describe them. Once I even went to the expense of buying a very good telescopic sight for my gun because I am not a very good shot. But it didn't improve things much – just frightened them off to the next farm along.

Now I must emphasize that I am very fond of birds, carrion crows apart. We've got some wonderful hawks around here, including peregrines nesting up the valley in Ullswater. The other summer I spent hours lying on my back watching three peregrines through my binoculars, a breeding pair and one youngster. Now that was a bonny day. There's also a golden eagle around this area at the moment. We've always had them in the Lake District and a golden eagle is so beautiful and distinctive that there is no mistaking them. In the past when they were more plentiful, the odd one got shot for taking lambs – not that I ever had any trouble – but now everybody wants to protect them and the bird society people try to keep their nests secret. That doesn't always work because I know one man in recent times who used to run guided tours for visitors to show them a golden eagle's nest.

In addition to the dippers and the sandpipers, another bird

appears to have become a casualty and that's the barn owl. I had a building down over the fields where, for at least twenty years to my knowledge, and probably long before that, barn owls would nest in the slates at the top of one wall. The chicks kept on tumbling out and I would put them in my pocket – just a ball of fluff they were – and climb up and put them back. Once most of the nest came down as well. So I thought I would sort it out once and for all, found a square post and fastened it right along the wall to keep the chicks and the nest safe.

I used to enjoy watching those owls, too, but sad to say they disappeared a few years ago and they've never been back.

Ullswater – practically an empty lake these days.

66

Eddie Pool and friends.

There was an eloquent last word on the whole sorry business from Eddie Pool.

I'm glad in a way that some of the old locals, the real Lakeland characters like my dad, didn't see the bad times. They were either too old or dead when it happened. There's a generation now who will never know about fishing and otters or terriers and hunting. They won't know what to look out for on the lake or on the shore, or how to sense the ways of nature.

It made a hell of a difference to me, though. It altered my life totally.

7

Cedric Robinson and the Wet Sahara

*P*roceed south and west from Ullswater, past the glories of Thirlmere, Grasmere, Coniston and Windermere and you arrive at a glistening, golden wilderness which has been aptly described as Britain's Wet Sahara. Depending, that is, on the state of the tide. When the tide is full, the place is simply Morecambe Bay, and no different to another thousand seascapes around this island of ours. But when the sea withdraws it leaves behind 120 square miles of treacherous sandbanks and dykes which have taken countless lives over the centuries. Morecambe Bay yields the justly famous shrimps – once exported round the world – as well as prime cockles, whitebait, the occasional salmon and the flook, a flatfish which is common in the area if you know where to look. On one side of the bay stands the holiday resort which gives it its name. On the other stands Flookburgh, named after the fish, where a group of uncompromising fishermen live and work. But they are not like other fishermen, for they do not put to sea in boats. Indeed, they wait until the tide recedes and then race out over the sands on their tractors, dragging trailers behind, to compete for the best spots along the dyke to trawl for shrimps and hunt for cockles.

Danger is ever present. When it does come in, the tide can outpace a galloping horse, and the unwary can be cut off and swept away. Then there are the quicksands, which can swallow a tractor as easily as you and I can take an aspirin. The area is studded with the graves of tractors – and people.

The men of Flookburgh and the surrounding area are tough, competitive, but entirely admirable. But one man stands out among them, a man with a very special responsibility and one who tends to go his own

'I liked him the moment I first saw him' – Cedric Robinson.

way. He is Cedric Robinson, the Queen's Guide, which is a proud and ancient title. Since 1963 he had led thousands of people safely from one side to the other, including royalty, and no one knows better than he the moods and hazards of this volatile area. Cedric became something of a celebrity when he emerged as the central character in Barry Cockcroft's film documentary, *Men of the Wet Sahara*, which won major international honours, including a United Nations Environment Programme Silver Medal. Then Cedric wrote a book, *Sand Pilot of Morecambe Bay*, which was so successful that it led to three more publications and an honorary degree from Lancashire Polytechnic.

So I knew about Cedric long before I met him. And I liked him even before we were introduced – which I will explain in a moment. I had been staying at Abbot Hall, a lovely hotel, run by the Methodist Holiday Guild in Grange-over-Sands, which is next door to Flookburgh, and

Fishing on the Wet Sahara.

had been told that Cedric wanted to meet me. Anyway, there I was in the reception area of Abbot Hall when in walked this man. At first I thought he was someone else I was due to meet but I really liked the look of him. He had an aura about him, and you just knew immediately he was one of nature's gentlemen. Eventually I found out who he was and we got on famously from the first meeting. Next day I went to see his place and meet his wife, a grand person who was once a beauty queen, and I was shown around the little farm they have, which is about ten acres. They have a couple of cows to breed from, a black and white pony, and had just acquired a goat which was going to be sent in for meat but Cedric got to hear and saved her. I think she will turn out to be a good milker. I really enjoyed myself, and came back again some time later because YTV's *Calendar* programme wanted to film Cedric and me out on the sands together. He took me out in a vehicle

Sunset over Morecambe Bay – and time to head for home.

(*top*) A chat with Cedric.

(*bottom*) Touring Cedric's smallholding.

he had specially made to carry passengers safely over the sands. It's like a little bus, with nice seats, which Cedric pulls along with a powerful tractor. I wasn't too thrilled at first when we started across the bay and I thought about those quicksands which I know alter position from day to day, but Cedric has the knowledge and I don't think he has lost a client yet!

I'd seen Hannah's films and Olive and I had always wanted to meet her – even talked about having a drive over to her place, but then thought better of it. She wouldn't have known us from Adam, and it was likely she would be pestered with lots of people. But one evening there was a knock on the door and in came Bill Mitchell, the author of all those books about the Yorkshire Dales, and the editor for many years of *The Dalesman* magazine. He said Hannah was in the area, and when I said how much I would like to shake her hand he fixed it with Mr David Mycock, the manager, for me to go to Abbot Hall. Hannah and I hit it off straight away and, the next day as she was returning home, it was Hannah who turned up on our

Signing a book for Olive Robinson.

doorstep. She was much taken by our smallholding and obviously related to our old-fashioned ways. Just like her we've always regarded our cattle as pets. Every time we go out to them they start mooing and you talk to them and you get to know their individual habits.

Hannah was very interested, borrowed a pair of wellies and we went on a wander around the fields. She kept offering me advice, saying that she hoped I didn't think she was interfering. But it was jolly good advice, based on a lifetime's experience. I have a nice cow which is a bit delicate and she was in calf during Hannah's first visit. It was a difficult birth because it turned out to be a big calf and we had to get the vet to pull it out. It was born live, but it died the next day. Of course, I had to explain all this when Hannah returned to do that bit of filming with me for Yorkshire Television and she told me that in my place she would put it to a smaller bull in future. She was very wise, and said that modern farming methods didn't always work and led to a lot of vet's bills, for Caesarean births and other problems. In the old days, nature used to take care of things. She suggested that we used a Hereford or an Aberdeen Angus next time and I agreed that it would be a good idea. Then she took a keen interest in the grass of my mowing meadow and volunteered to come back at haytime to help!

That trip we had out on the sands during the second visit turned out to be quite an adventure. I'm pretty sure Hannah enjoyed herself and I was delighted to give her a ride in my vehicle, which I call the Sandpiper. But by the time we had got everything organized and ready for the film crew the tide was coming in, and we couldn't go out very far. In fact, it began chasing us back and I kept telling the film crew we couldn't stay much longer, but they wanted their interview. Then when we turned to go back, there was hell up, because it was coming in alongside us. Hannah said, 'Oh! – you did say that the tide came in very quickly and you are right!'

But we weren't in any danger. I'm far too cautious to take risks because I know those sands. I was born to the place, like my father and grandfather and probably several generations back. Getting a living from the sands was the only thing we ever thought of doing. When I left school to start work there would be fifty men with horses and carts, all setting off together, crossing the river at Humphrey Head and then going at a full trot in a line sweeping into the distance. In my dad's time there were twice as many. When we got to the shrimping ground it would be every man for himself, and the nets would be thrown into the dykes to trawl for shrimps.

Cedric, setting off for the sands.

I lived in a cottage in Flookburgh which was so small that I had to sleep in the same room as my mother and father, since we only had two bedrooms and my sisters slept in the other. Like Hannah, we had no electricity or running water and lit our way to bed with candles. I was the only boy, and I went everywhere with my father, hardly left his side. When the Second World War came some fishermen managed to become exempt from the forces but for some reason they took my father. I was six or seven at the time and I still remember him telling me as we were sitting on the top step together outside the cottage. I sobbed my eyes out – they just couldn't con-

Picking a way through the perils of Morecambe Bay in Sandpiper One.

trol me. Anyway, I got used to it after a while. He was away for four years, serving in Egypt and Italy, but the main thing was he survived. Somehow my mother had managed to save enough to buy a good horse so we could start fishing again on his return. When I left school at the age of fourteen we began to run three horses, and had to mow the grass verges for hay because we had no land.

The bigger and more powerful the horse the more chance you had on the fishing grounds. Because if you got in deep with a little horse you'd be crying glad to get out. Sometimes there was no choice but to go deep, but though a horse can swim and pull a cart it can't drag a net as well. Often you would be waist deep in water and only the head and the ears of your horse would be showing, and if it got into trouble you had to release the net or the horse would drown.

Now and again things would go badly wrong, as it did once for Les Butler, who appeared in that television programme with me – sadly he is dead now. Les had a very excitable horse, and he and a pal called Herbert, who had his own horse and cart, crossed the river on the hardest side one day. They got out of their depth and when they turned to move out of trouble and join the rest of us in a

Scenes from the old days, when shrimping required a good horse.

better place, Herbert's horse was all right and swam steadily to safety. But Les's horse panicked, started lunging up and down, flung Les out of the cart, trapping his legs in a rope. Fortunately he managed to shake free of his boots and the current took him to our side where he was picked up. But the horse just kept swimming round and round in circles, tightening the rope, and drowned. Aye, that was a bad do.

But we all looked after our horses. My dad always told me to be mindful of their welfare because it was a long way home without one. It can get so cold out there, so the first thing we would do when we got back to shore was to take the horse out of the shafts, face the cart into the wind for its protection, put its blanket on and give it a feed. Only then would we get on with the work of sorting out the shrimps or whatever it was we were bringing in.

You had more cause to be grateful to your horse than just the day-to-day work it did. We would be able to go out in mist and fog because of an extra sense they possessed. Fog is the worst thing out in the bay because, if you cannot see, all the knowledge and experience about the tides and quicksands is pretty near wiped out. But if you left a trail by dragging an old sack with a weight attached the horse would follow that trail back home again however bad a night it was, or however thick the fog. You couldn't see it, but the horse could, or at least sense it – and you would just sit there and depend on it totally.

Not all horses are reliable, however. One I remember never got accustomed to the feel of sand beneath it. On hard ground it was all right, but when it felt its hooves going down an inch or two it would move forward. Most horses you could train to stay still, but this one never got the hang of it. After a week or two of trying and failing, the fisherman who had bought it realized it would never be any good for, say, cockling when the horse would stand loose. One night they went to check their nets for flooks and it left them – ran off with their cart. They couldn't catch it whatever they tried, and ended up walking home, believing it to be swept away by the tide and they would never see horse nor cart again. Anyway, the horse was found alive on the promenade at Grange-over-Sands the next day, having been out all night. It had found the strength to break free and still had the two shafts of the cart attached to it, which may have helped it to keep afloat.

The horses have been replaced by tractors, of course, and quite a few of those have gone down in the quicksands over the years. But no fisherman has been lost in my lifetime. They usually go out in groups, which is a kind of insurance if you do hit a snag. But there was one incident a couple of years ago when one man went off on his own and his tractor broke down as the tide began to come to the flood. He was lucky. He stood on his tractor, took off his yellow oil-skin and waved it. The others were about three miles away but they spotted him and came for him. Otherwise he would have lost his life as well as his tractor because there is no walking back when you are that far out as the tide turns. It covers that 120 square miles at a frightening speed.

Fishermen are aware of this, but most of the general public are not. I don't think it's any exaggeration to say there have been hundreds of tragedies, stretching back centuries, and they go on to this day.

For instance, four teenagers began to stroll along Hest Bank one summer's night. Two stuck with the coastline but the other two struck out across the bay. That night there was a ten metre tide and where they went the sea comes up under the Morecambe side and cuts you off, and that's what happened to them. There was a big police search in which I was involved, except I never moved from the house – just gave advice on the phone to the police to tell them where I thought their bodies would be found, working on the wind direction and what I knew about the movement of sand in that particular area.

Well, I came home the next evening and found a couple sitting there in the house waiting for me. It turned out to be the parents of one of the boys. The sad thing was, the body of his mate had been found the day before but there was no sign of their son. They had been out all day with the police, scouring the shoreline. So we sat and talked, and it was very upsetting. They said they could not understand how he had drowned because he was such a marvellous swimmer, so I told them it would have made no difference out there and it would have been all over in ten minutes.

There was the question of his body, of course. The bay usually gives up its dead on the third day, so when the police rang again for advice on the last day of the search I told them to look in a certain area. Sure enough, they found him. His body was almost buried, and in another day would have been completely covered. It would probably have been another twelve months before there was a chance of it reappearing. I got a letter of thanks from the police after that.

I always remember talking to a lady in her nineties who told me that when she was a young girl she was helping her father work the sands for cockles when a glove suddenly appeared. Her dad started to dig round it and found there was a body attached to it.

There would be all sorts of things under those sands, including aeroplanes. I understand a Spitfire tried to come down here during the war and has never been seen since. One very misty day several years ago I heard a plane out there getting nearer and nearer and then suddenly there was a thud – then silence. Some fishermen tried to get to it but they were prevented by the tide. When they did find it, the pilot had obviously died on crashing because nearly every bone in his body was broken. But even had he survived the impact, he would have drowned.

However, there was one exceptionally lucky man that the bay didn't get. He was a bird-watcher who went out on the promenade at Grange with his binoculars, and thought he saw puffins. Well, we don't have puffins in Morecambe Bay, but we do have oyster-

An asthmatic boy is rescued from the deadly quicksands.

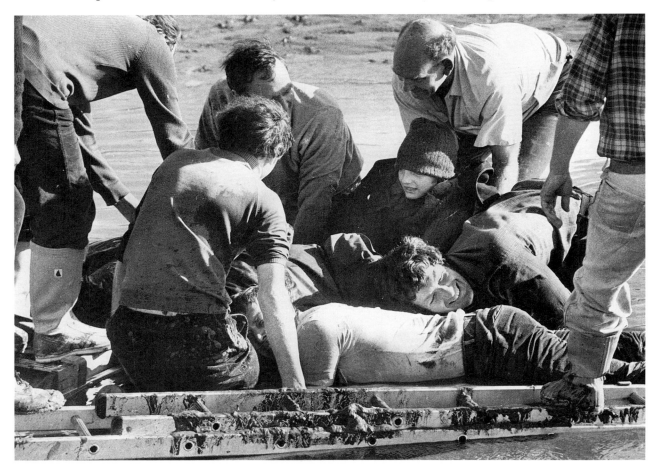

catchers, which are black and white, and that's what he must have seen. The birds were on the river's edge quite a way out, and off he set. By the time he got there the tide was coming in fast, and when he tried to get back he was cut off. Luckily, a woman in Grange saw him and dialled 999 for the coastguard. Now, I am a member of that organization so they telephoned me to see if I could see anyone on the sandbank. But by the time I put the phone down and got my glasses out, those sandbanks were gone, all underwater. They launched an inflatable boat at Arnside with two men on board to go and look for him and I listened to them on my radio. They went backwards and forwards for almost two hours but the visibility was bad and the water a bit rough. In the end I asked someone to get in touch with the woman who had reported it in the first place, to try and give them a direct line on the sighting. They were told it was from the playing fields at Grange to the church in Silverdale, so they said that as a last resort they would sail along this line, cut the engines, shout and listen. On the third time they did this, they heard a faint voice crying 'Help!'. There he was. There were a number of factors which helped to save that man. First of all, he was a big, strapping bloke and a good swimmer. Secondly, he had got between two flows which had created an eddy, and kept him in one place. Thirdly, he was wearing a jacket which fastened round his middle like an oilskin, and some air had got in and helped to keep him afloat.

Every year there's two or three. People see the sunshine, and the sands dry out very invitingly at low tide. So they go out that little bit further. Even locals, who should know, get into trouble. One summer, a family who had lived round here all their lives went for a stroll on the sands. There were a lot of them, seven or eight including a toddler, and they went down in the quicksands. All, that is, except the lightweight toddler who managed to wriggle free. They were terrified, of course, because they thought that the tide would come in and drown them. But that day it was a low tide, the sands had been piled high and they were only a hundred yards from shore. It was the little one who ran to the shore to fetch help, so that one ended happily as well. But there was a terrible incident for some local lads, just teenagers, who went riding their motor bikes through a gulley on the sand. But the sand softened up and one got stuck on his brand new bike, only up to his knees. First of all his mates thought he was larking about, but when the water comes in that stuff can set like cement. They soon realized it was serious and went to get help, but by then the tide was on its way in. And

(*overleaf*) The start of a quiet stroll across Morecambe Bay! (*bottom left*): The fisherfolk of Flookborough, circa 1920. (*bottom right*): A damp patch along the way!

though they and the fire brigade tried everything they could to free him it was no use. The last thing they did for the poor lad was to give him a fireman's breathing apparatus and leave him. But the air must have run out and he drowned.

Since then they have developed methods which are designed to help release people trapped in the quicksands. The coastguards use a pump to push water around their limbs to loosen up the sand, and this method was used successfully to release an asthmatic lad within a couple of hours. The fire brigade prefer to pump down compressed air which they say has the same effect. Either way, you have to hope the tide isn't due in soon.

My main job now is to see people safely across from one side of the bay to the other, so I have to be out all the time sizing the job up. It's the River Kent that governs it, and it moves every day as the wind and the tides shift the sandbanks around. I have known it move a distance of four miles overnight! In the days before they had the comfort of railways, people could save a lot of time going across Morecambe Bay so there were regular stage coach services and foot traffic. As the crow flies, it might be four or five miles across, but I've never known the time when you could go straight across. You can end up doing about ten miles.

But it's a lot further going round the coast route, so travellers naturally looked towards the locals for assistance when they tried crossing. The first royal appointment was in the early thirteen hundreds and prior to that there would be unofficial guides. At first they were associated with Cartmel Priory. Maybe even the abbots themselves tried to help, but it would have been mostly guesswork in those days. A lot of lives were lost, a hundred in fact, according to the priory records. I was appointed guide thirty years ago and moved from Flookburgh to Guides Farm at Grange. The place and the smallholding comes with the job, but not much else. The annual honorarium is £15 and there is no charge for being guided across the sands. Some people are generous, some just say, 'Thank you very much, Mr Robinson,' and that's it. Looking back at the history of the official guides I discovered that at one time they were allowed to sell ale to travellers to make a bit extra. But I had to do the job in between working as a fisherman and, my goodness, that can be a very competitive business. It's necessary for them to keep within sight of each other for the sake of safety, but there's not much pleasant conversation. For instance, if one finds a good bed of cockles he will try his best to keep it to himself, and shrimping can create some heated arguments. Feuds have been known to spring up between the different families and last a generation. There have been several fist-fights at the sands and legend says that one man had his ear bitten off in one scrap.

Shrimping became so cut-throat that I gave it up to go off on my own, netting for flooks, and cockling. As long as I earn enough to make a living I am content. But fishing in Morecambe Bay has been in decline for the last ten years and there is even a definite fall in demand for the shrimps, despite their reputation for being the best there is. I heard recently that the Fishermen's Society in Flook-burgh, which markets shrimps, still had half the previous year's catch unsold. People may be worried about the possibility of pollution from Sellafield further up the coast, and at the moment we are fighting a scheme to pump sewage from Blackpool and Fleetwood out into the lower reaches of the bay.

Cedric nets a flook.

Cockling in Morecambe Bay, a hundred years ago . . .

. . . and Cedric uses exactly the same technique today.

Then a couple of years ago catching flooks became uncommercial, so I had to look round for something else to do to earn a bit of money.

A friend of mine offered to build a trailer for passengers, which I could hook on to the tractor and give rides to people across the sands. So we did it. I called it 'Sandpiper One', and we had some fun, although the snag was it had no great protection from the elements. When the showers came I had to turn this way and that so that passengers shared the worst of the weather on the windward side. We even had two ninety-year-olds go out with us, but we wrapped them up well in blankets, and do you know they said it

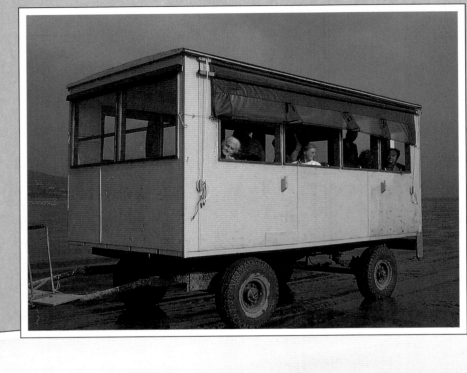

A ride for me on Sandpiper Two (*left and opposite*).

. . . a more protected vehicle than Sandpiper One (*bottom*).

was the best day out they could recall in all the years they had been coming to this area on holiday.

Now I have 'Sandpiper Two', which is much bigger and with more seats and - most importantly – sides to keep out the weather. But they lift up if it is sunny.

One day I took out twenty nuns, all dressed in their habits, and they wanted to go to the Holy Well at St Agnes, which springs out from the rocks. It is supposed to be good for what ails you, particularly rheumatics. When I was a nipper, a corrugated building covered it and they used to bottle it and sell to the holidaymakers on the promenade at Morecambe. Nowadays there is no building, the trees have grown all round it and you could pass by without knowing it was there. Obviously, it has some religious significance which is probably why the nuns wanted to see it. When we arrived, the sand was a bit too wet for walking across dressed the way they were, so they asked me to go and fill up three flasks for them. They said they would save two to take back to a nursing home, but the other one they passed round one to the other to sample as we rode back.

The fishing may be bad now, and there are very few Flookburgh men at it full time these days, but they still come from far and wide to cross the sands. When I was first appointed I thought I was doing well if thirty people turned up, but it's different now. 'Sandpiper Two' is very busy, and hundreds more want to go on foot. Some of them are very determined. I once had a booking from a big group – around 250 – but when I turned up to meet them at Arnside it was hardly fit because of mist and rain. So I put it to them – did they really want to go out to such a hazardous place in conditions like that? But they said they did. So I told them to keep close behind me and we struck out. Visibility was down to 80 yards, which isn't far on a ten-mile walk. You have to read the sands and follow the river down to where you think it will be safe. Olive, my wife, happened to be at Kents Bank railway station at the time, and she could hear us talking right out in the bay. My, but she was glad to see us arrive that day, and I was pretty pleased to see the shore myself.

However, that was nothing to compare to the time I took the Duke of Edinburgh across in 1985, driving a coach with a four-in-hand. I was told to find as secluded a route as I could for security reasons, and I was out looking and testing for a long time in advance. But three days before the big event conditions became so bad that all I could do was hope. I was marking the course of the River Kent with laurel bushes and found it was moving three hundred yards with each tide. Then I started getting some unusual phone calls from locals, and even from further afield. They were very worried for me, asking what would happen if I got Prince Philip stuck in the quicksands. Would I be sent to prison?

Luckily the weather took a turn for the better, the river sorted itself out and the sand dried out. But a lot of people were still worried, including the Chief Coastguard who saw me checking one soft spot and said I was surely never thinking of bringing him through that. I told him I would, if it was possible.

I was out there at three in the morning on the day itself, arriving at the river at first light. I was delighted to see it had moved on to hard ground. Everything looked good, but there was no way I was going to become careless. It was the first horse-drawn carriage crossing of that kind for over a hundred years. And when I arrived to meet the royal party I found to my horror that the route for the start of the run had become terrible. There were twelve carriages all riding round eager to go, and one of the Prince's friends called out 'Come on Mr Robinson, let's go!' And I told him I must have a word with the drivers first, because they weren't going to drive across just any old sand and I was responsible. So they all stood round me in a circle and I told them that to begin with it would only be safe to ride six carriages abreast. I was still trying to weigh up the situation and get everyone into place when the Prince turned to me and said 'Come on, Mr Robinson – we're going to be here all day!' So I thought, just wait until you get out on those sands and you will find out a bit about the dangers. But when we got going he was very good and he asked me lots and lots of questions. It turned out to be a wonderful day, really.

The hardest part was to come, however – trying to slow the Prince down. I wanted them to trot across the soft sand and walk the rest of the way. But he had something different in mind, and got the whip going. So I looked at my watch and said: 'Sir, do you mind slowing the team down?' He rather snapped at me: 'What for, Mr Robinson?' I had to explain that we had to cross over some railway lines at the end of the ride, and they had laid some lovely new boards over the lines so that the horses wouldn't be frightened – and there was a train due in. He said that surely they would stop the b— train. But I was also concerned about the dignitaries waiting there to shake his hand – I'd never seen so many in one place before.

After the stop at the station he was supposed to go to a farm where they had made arrangements to have the carriages hosed down while the mud they had collected was still wet. But what did he do – drive straight past the farm and all the way to Holker Hall, where he was staying! No security, no police, anything, and two helicopters had been on duty. He left them all behind.

Now that was an unnerving experience, but four years later there was worse to come. Lancashire Polytechnic decided to grant me an honorary degree in Physics and Science – me, who had left school at fourteen – saying it was for the outstanding contribution I had given to the people of Lancashire over the last thirty years.

The ceremony was at the Guildhall in Preston. Well, you had to enter to a fanfare of trumpets in front of six hundred people and listen to your citation, which seemed to go on for hours.

I had to make a reply, and normally that doesn't worry me because I am often asked to talk to various groups and do it without any notes. But this time I jotted a few things down on bits of cardboard.

Do you know, for the very first time in my life I was nervous. Shaking like a leaf, I was.

8

A Favoured Form of Travel

*T*ravel is now one of my chief delights. After being starved of it for sixty years I suppose I am making up for lost time, being on the move most days as various invitations to go hither and thither pour in, and it's fortunate that an inclination I had in my younger days to suffer from travel sickness seems to have gone away. I was worried it may return when I faced up to my first ocean crossing, as I travelled to Europe for the *Innocent Abroad* television series. There were no problems, even though a force 7 gale was blowing. Later on, I went across the Irish Sea to be a guest on a television show in Belfast, and became somewhat concerned about the reputation of that particular stretch of water, which is said to be much fiercer than the English Channel. I felt a touch queasy on the way back home, but a breath of fresh air sorted me out, so I can now claim to be a fairly seasoned ocean voyager.

Flying is a different matter. I have not been able to contemplate boarding an aircraft up to now, but circumstances may now one day oblige me to reconsider the situation seriously. If I do any more foreign travel for television in the *Innocent Abroad* manner, for instance, then it will obviously become an issue. Not that I dug my heels in and refused to fly for the first series – merely requested that such a form of travel be avoided. I like trains, don't mind cars, can tolerate boats, but the prospect of hurtling through the air at a vast speed does not appeal.

Of that list, trains offer the most comfortable and appealing way of travel, or so I thought until quite recently. But I have made a discovery which has definitely revised that opinion. It all came about when I was motoring around the North, visiting bookshops for signing sessions of my previous publications, and I stayed the night at a place on the A6 between Preston and Lancaster called Bilsborrow, which is only a few

miles south from Morecambe Bay and Cedric Robinson. The hotel is called Olde Duncombe House, a very pleasant and happy place, but the really significant point about it is its position.

Directly alongside a canal.

It was pure chance that brought me to Olde Duncombe House, but it has left me a lasting impression because I have fallen in love with the concept of canal travel. It suits me perfectly. The narrowboats are romantic, and glide gently along in such a tranquil way through the countryside at a speed of 2½ miles an hour. And the depth of water is

A chat with Alec Bolton on his narrowboat.

'. . . shall we go for a trip?'

often so shallow that if it became necessary you could step off in the middle of the canal and wade safely to the nearest bank.

A comforting thought for a nervous old thing like me!

This enthusiasm was kindled by the kindness of the proprietor of the hotel, Alex Bolton, who has been involved with canal boats since his young days. Moored right next to his premises on the Lancaster Canal was his own narrowboat, 60 feet long, 11 feet wide and, since it was only built in 1986, superbly appointed with every convenience you could think of. Indeed, when the hotel was being developed out of three cottages and a derelict barn, Alex and his wife, Jane, and their young children, lived very happily on it for well over three years.

During the last couple of years I have arranged travel plans to ensure that I stay with Alex and his family whenever possible – around half a dozen times up to now – and have spent hours on the boat. Not that I have travelled far along the canal – just a couple of miles or so – but it has given me a taste for more. In fact, I may even book a canal holiday one day, if the opportunity arises.

Alex has been interested in canal boats ever since the fifties, when he was working as an apprentice radio and television engineer and his boss bought an old boat and sent him down to do some work on it. Alex has enjoyed an interesting and varied career, and is the son of an extremely unusual lady. Lizzie Bolton was the captain of a very famous ladies' football team based in Preston and run by a man called Dick Kerr, which played in the 1920s. Alex says it became the best ladies' team in the world, and his mother travelled to play in France and even the United States. Apparently, ladies' football became very popular in that time and could draw crowds of over fifty thousand. He showed me photographs of his mother and her team and said there had been plenty of film shot of the matches, by the *Pathé Newsreel* and others. Some had been featured on television recently.

But it seems that the sporting careers of Mrs Bolton and her team-

Mrs Lizzie Bolton, Alec's mother, is seated, next to the end on the right.

THE FAMOUS PRESTON LADIES' F.C. LATE DICK KERR LADIES' F.C. AT ROYAL LANCASHIRE SHOW 1933.

mates came to an abrupt end. According to her son, the Football Association put a stop to it in the 1930s because they were concerned that the women were attracting larger attendances than the men! However, the female influence in football appears to be making a comeback because I hear there are many thriving and enthusiastic teams of ladies playing today. Alex told me that they compete in a national championship each year held in the Preston area, and some of the teams book into his place, which I think is very fitting under the circumstances.

Alex has had something of an adventurous life himself. After two or three jobs in his youth, he joined the Military Police and then became a fireman, and later on a radio and television engineer before deciding eight years ago to build his hotel, basically from scratch. I'm not surprised he chose to locate it where he did because all through those years he maintained an affection for canals. And he has such a poetic way of describing them, as he will tell you.

Lizzie Bolton scores a goal.

I call them the diamonds in our midst. It's rather like the story of the old farmer in South Africa who found the Hope Diamond while working his land, not realizing over the years as he dug around the dirt that one of the most famous gems in the world was lurking there. That's a fair analogy for Britain's canals. They have been around for generations, dirty and neglected, but they are a major asset for the whole community to enjoy.

The reason for the decline in our canals is summed up in a nutshell by the very one I live alongside, the Lancaster Canal, which links Preston to Lancaster. It was built around the end of the eighteenth century, but was never linked up to the main canal system because the railways came. Everything was in place for the connection, but the competition was too much and it was abandoned. Nevertheless, it was well used in its day. Because they were both on coastal rivers, Preston and Lancaster were very rich merchant towns. Lancaster was even prominent in the slave trade, because thousands of the poor souls were brought there before being shipped on to America.

Anyway, there was an urgent need for a safe way to proceed between the two towns. Before they dug the canal, the top businessmen had two choices – go by road or by sea. Both options had their perils – the sea for obvious reasons, and the road because it was infested with highwaymen. Either way they risked their wallets or their necks, or both. When the canal finally became operational, the people who ran it were very enterprising. They offered what I understand was a unique service – an express canal barge. The merchants could do the journey from Preston to Lancaster and on to Kendal in one day on a boat pulled by a team of horses. Every ten miles or so they would have a fresh lot of horses ready to take over and keep the speed up.

There was a big trade along this route. The northern part wanted the coal from the pits in Lancashire and the south needed the stone from the quarries around Kendal. All the stone used in the properties out of which I built the hotel was originally dragged out of the bottom of the River Brock, which shows how desperate they must have been for the stuff. Incidentally, most of the timbers came from the wrecks of ships along the coast, which is only around ten miles away and points out the dangers of seafaring in the seventeenth and eighteenth centuries.

It's a pity they didn't carry on and join up the Lancaster Canal with the main network, although there was still an outlet to the sea at Glasson. There are still 43 navigable miles along our canal, and I know every inch of it but it still sadly limits my horizons. You can't just haul a 60-foot boat out of the water and put it on a trailer!

When I first met Jane I took her to York for a holiday by canal. Naturally, we had to hire another boat from Chorley, which is only just down the road. Nine boats with 36 people went on that trip, and it was memorable. Non-stop for two weeks, negotiating 144 locks across the Pennines, and the same number back again. We sailed right through the centre of Leeds on the way to York which we reached on the Saturday lunchtime, a week after setting off. Since we only had a fortnight to spare, there was just time for one night out in York before leaving on Sunday morning to make sure we got back in time.

For me, the canals spell freedom. If I ever pack up working, I'll become a travelling man, permanently cruising the countryside of Britain.

Period postcard of Deep Cutting Bridge on the Lancaster Canal.

9

The Emerald Dale

When you leave the Lancaster Canal and head out east, within ten minutes you are on the fringe of my own land – the Yorkshire Dales. Go north a little and you arrive at the threshold of what is certainly another jewel in the northern crown.

Wensleydale can justifiably claim to be the best-known and most celebrated of all the Yorkshire dales and if the canals are the diamond, then Wensleydale is the emerald in our midst. It is best entered through Sedbergh, a splendid old town which I first visited many years ago to attend a sheep auction with Uncle Tommy, and chanced to find an inscription which, for me, sums up Wensleydale. A dales auction is a man's world, so I slipped away to have a wander and found a house with a stone verandah on which were carved the words:

I will lift up mine eyes to the hills

This has always stuck in my mind, and it is certainly an appropriate message, for nowhere else in Yorkshire will you see such a wealth and variety of different hills glowing every variety of green, particularly when they reflect the late afternoon sun. The splendour of Wensleydale may be matched elsewhere along the Pennine chain, but never surpassed. And there is more of it, too, for it stretches from Sedbergh, all the way down to Leyburn and beyond.

The road from Sedbergh to Hawes encompasses in an abbreviated form the full glory of the Yorkshire Dales. Every yard of the fifteen miles between the two towns is absorbing, almost like a roll of film with scene following splendid scene without pause. Away to the left you will, perhaps, see a team of black-and-white border collies ushering 100 or more sheep across a difficult fell top, leaping ditches and walls, and running until their lungs come close to bursting, responding to the

Wensleydale . . . The Emerald Dale.

whistles and shouts of a shepherd. If you are sharp of eye you may spot him, a tiny figure hurrying across the fields to try and keep pace. But for every mile he travels, his dogs will travel ten. Then the picture will change dramatically into a beautiful kind of desolation, hundreds of acres stretching to the horizon where nothing is happening and nothing much is moving except, maybe, a frightened hare racing through the heather, or, if you are very fortunate, a vixen scouting for that night's supper. Where long-neglected stone barns shed roof slates around their feet and few trees have the strength and stamina to withstand the torment of winter.

Small communities, hamlets really, occasionally appear, built in the lee of the fell for shelter and usually close by a bend of the stream

which cuts along the bottom of Upper Wensleydale. Cottages weathered by centuries of wind, rain and sun, with gardens stoutly walled to give the plants and flowers a chance of survival. Very occasionally, there are shops of the kind my mother would have been comfortable with, and at regular intervals a Methodist chapel. That there is only one public house along the entire fifteen miles of this enchanted route demonstrates the solemn power the Methodists once possessed hereabouts.

Just over half-way between the two towns is an obscure road which leads to a dale, which was at one and the same time the saddest and one of the loveliest in the North Country. Grisedale, a tributary valley nestling half a mile away over a rise, is too insignificant to be mentioned by many popular maps, yet it was once the kind of dale that romantic poets dreamt about. Enclosed by the wildly dramatic fells of Upper Wensleydale and peopled by a thriving, basic but happy community with a schoolhouse and a chapel and all the space and freedom anyone could wish for, a place unpolluted in the complete sense of the word, since the more doubtful influences and pressures of society at large scarcely touched it. The Romans had hunted wild boar on Grisedale's upper reaches – as the name Wild Boar Fell, and a shrine to Sylvanus, the god of the savage lands, still surviving just to the northeast testify – and the farms and dwellings were, without exception, built to a traditional Viking design. Such an absorbing history the place must have known down the centuries and, small though it was, every imaginable form of human expression in all its infinite variety.

The twentieth century took a long time to make its presence felt in Grisedale, but when it did it was fatal. Market forces and depressions broke down the old, self-supporting system and one by one the families left. The farmsteads were abandoned to the mercy of the elements, the schoolhouse closed down, to be followed later by the chapel.

Grisedale was left to die. In the mid-seventies only one farm survived, run by a valiant ex-miner called Joe Gibson. Most of the others, fifteen in all, just collapsed into picturesque ruins, mere scars on the fellside. Eight were eventually converted into holiday homes, which breathed some life back into this valley, but the fighting spirit of the Vikings vanished when Joe Gibson died and his son eventually left Mouse Syke Farm. There is no working farm left now in Grisedale.

Barry Cockcroft became totally absorbed with Grisedale during the early seventies and spent long months researching every farm and every family as far back as written records and the memories of the local elders would go. It led to his book, *The Dale That Died*, now one

Springtime in the Emerald Dale – Joe Gibson inspects the new crop of lambs.

(*top*) Joe Gibson of Grisedale rescues a sheep from the river.

(*bottom*) Joe branding a Swaledale tup.

Joe Gibson and his friend, Chris Pratt, alongside one of the abandoned farms in Grisedale.

of the most hunted literary works in the North since every copy sold and it is long out of print, and the celebrated film of the same name. Both featured the indomitable Joe Gibson, and his friend, Chris Pratt, the molecatcher of Grisedale, born and raised in the place and another memorable character. I met them both years ago, but neither is with us now, alas.

However, returning back over the rise to the remainder of this mesmeric route, from the entrance of Grisedale to Hawes is a mere six miles. But, when all the farms of Grisedale were alive with the clamour of rural toil well over half a century ago, communications between the two places were minimal. A horse and cart would collect produce around the dale once a week to take to market in Hawes, but most

The river running along
the bottom of the
Emerald Dale.

people were too busy with their labours or lacked the inclination to travel.

Hawes is the capital of Upper Wensleydale, and almost a bustling metropolis when compared to Grisedale. By the turn of the century it had been invaded by industry, the railway, commerce and a thriving auction mart. Yet Hawes always clung tenaciously to the old country ways, and still does. You may find it difficult today to cross the road or even walk easily along the pavement during the seething weeks of the season, but all you need to do to escape in the spiritual sense is to lift up your eyes to the hills, for there they are, in splendid array all around the town. Even when the madding crowds obscure the essential meaning of the place you can still see, if you care to look, that the main thrust of life is, as it was and always has been, pivoted on what the fells will yield – the daily gallonage of milk and the annual crop of sheep and cattle.

The character and attitudes of the people of Hawes are also as changeless as the landscape, demonstrably in the way they speak. The local patois remains stubbornly untouched by the influence of what

(*opposite*) Lift up your
eyes . . . an aerial view of
Hawes.

they listen to every day on the radio and television, and you instinctively realize that the way they speak is an outward and important assertion of their identity, a flag to be proudly flown at all times. A classic example of this spirit of patriotism came from the pen of the legendary Kit Calvert, unquestionably the most celebrated Dalesman of his time, who 'translated' biblical passages into Wensleydale dialect. For instance, the 23rd psalm goes like this:

> *The Lord is my Shipperd*
> *Ah'll want fer nowt.*
> *He lets m'bassock i' t' best pastur an taks m'*
> *bi t' watter side whar o's wyet on peeaceful.*
> *He uplifts mi sould, an' makes things seea easy 'at*
> *Ah can dew whats reet an' Gloryfy His neeame,*
> *Even if ah git t'deeaths deaursteead ahs nut be freetened,*
> *fer He'll bi wi mi,*
> *His cruek an' esh plant 'll up hod mi,*
> *Thoo puts a good meal afoor mi,*
> *Reet anenst them' at upbraids mi,*
> *Thoo ceuls mi heead wi' oil,*
> *An Ah've meeat an' drink t' spar'.*
> *Seurlie Thi goodness an' mercy 'al bi mine*
> *Fer o't days o' mi life*
> *An Ah'll beleng t' t'hoose o' the Lord fer ivver.*

(*top*) Kit Calvert, archetypal Dalesman. (*bottom*) Kit dressed for Buckingham Palace to collect his OBE.

Kit Calvert was such an extraordinary man. He had the talent, personality and the energy to succeed in any society and he managed to make a national impact despite being born in humble circumstances in an obscure rural area. The son of an impoverished quarry worker in the village of Burtersett, a community between Hawes and Bainbridge, he left school at twelve to go into farm service for four shillings a week. Then he launched out on his own with five leased acres – just five! – which could support four cows. He ended up as Managing Director of Wensleydale Creameries in Hawes, justifiably credited for saving it and the world-famous cheese from extinction. Would he were around today!

Kit had the ability to take on the top businessmen from the City, winning arguments around polished boardroom tables, yet he never abandoned his roots, remaining a true Dalesman – no, the complete Dalesman, clay pipe clenched in his teeth, until the end of his days. He was awarded the OBE, and when he died in his eighties his life was celebrated in the national press.

Arm in arm with Kit outside the byre at Low Birk Hatt.

Kit found the time to be a literary man, publishing his writings and running a distinctive second-hand bookshop in the centre of Hawes as a hobby during his retirement, which had an unusual sales policy. If, as often happened, Kit was absent on business, customers could still select a book and leave the money in a box on the table. Such a trusting man. The bookshop is still in business by the way.

I first met Kit in 1973 when he came to Cotherstone for the launch of Barry Cockcroft's first book, in which we both feature. Later on he came to visit me at Low Birk Hatt more than once, and I treasure a photograph of the two of us together outside my byre.

I thought him a marvellous man, and I wish circumstances would have allowed me the time to get better acquainted. But it was such a privilege to have known him personally at all. One of the main characteristics of Kit was his sense of humour. He was fun to be with, and had a stock of stories reflecting the wit and rural wisdom of the people of Wensleydale. I think this chapter should conclude with one of his best, in the words of the man himself.

A happy gathering, taken twenty years ago . . . (*top, left to right*): Me, Barry Cockcroft, Joe Gibson. (*seated l to r*): Kit Calvert, Mrs Jenny Gibson, Chris Pratt.

112

A Wensleydale
landscape.

It was when the chequebook first made an appearance in Wensleydale – it even preceded the telephone. One local man who farmed in
a big way was called Willy Pratt, who often went to Scotland to buy
stock, and he quickly realized the advantages of not having to carry
large wads of money about his person. Willy started life as a poor
farmer, but grew so powerful that he was the only man in Wensleydale who could make the Scottish Express stop especially for him at
Hawes. He was such a good customer, you see, able to fill a cattle
train on his own, so they didn't dare affront him. Off he went one
day with his chequebook to a major sale in Scotland, bought a lot of
stock and signed a lot of cheques. But a rumour started going
round, started no doubt by some malicious rivals of Willy's, that the

English banks were failing and not honouring cheques. Willy found himself besieged by Scottish breeders waving bits of paper and demanding a return of their cattle, which had already been driven down to the station for railing back to Hawes.

He turned for help to a friend, called Anthony Moore, another major cattle dealer in Wensleydale. Mr Moore said he might be able to assist, and took Willy into the stable of one of the local hotels where no one could see them. Then he pulled up one trouser leg to reveal a very thick woollen stocking, which he peeled back. Wrapped around his leg were rolls and rolls of banknotes tied with bits of string. He extracted four thousand pounds from his leg and gave them to Willy saying: 'Will that see ye through?'

'Yes, that'll git me through all right,' replied Willy when he had recovered from his amazement. 'But what about you, Anthony?'

Anthony just winked, tapped his other leg and said: 'I nobbut un-wrapped one leg, have I!'

10

The Story of a Second Son of Wensleydale

Two or three miles out of Hawes, the road running westwards along Upper Wensleydale arrives at Bainbridge, considered by many to be the most attractive village in a land full of traditional architectural beauty. Bainbridge has seemingly remained unchanged for a century or more, has a generously proportioned village green with the old stocks still surviving and is bordered on one side by a set of small waterfalls of considerable charm.

But for me, the people who inhabit a place are far more important than a picture postcard come to life, and Bainbridge was enhanced immeasurably by one man who, in a sense, presided over the place for many years. Go into the bar of the Rose and Crown, an historic inn which bestrides the upper part of the village, and you will see a modest memorial to the man, which I am sure would have pleased him a great deal. It is a small brass plaque, set into a high, spindle-backed chair strategically situated between the open fire and the bar, and it reads:

In fond memory of Dick Chapman, 1895-1981

Dick Chapman in his prime.

Dick Chapman was a schoolteacher. Now there are many thousands of teachers and most of them are very good at educating children, but every now and then one will emerge as a truly inspirational figure, one who will change the lives of scores of people with each succeeding generation of pupils who pass through his or her sphere of influence: a person who will ignite the aspirations of boys and girls who, in different hands, will almost certainly have led less fulfilled lives; a person who can identify potential in a youngster, draw it out, nurture it and paint a compelling picture of the life that youngster can expect to lead by pursuing education to the highest possible level.

In a sense, Dick was merely repaying – in more than full measure – a debt he owed to a teacher he himself was extremely fortunate to meet at a crucial stage in his life, who radically changed his own perspective of the future.

Dick taught in schools in the north-east and the West Riding of Yorkshire before returning to his beloved Wensleydale on retirement. Like Kit Calvert, his contemporary, he was a four-square Dalesman, a skilled fisherman who became the water bailiff of Bainbridge when his teaching career was over. And he was a weaver of legendary tales about the history, customs and characters of the rivers and fells, particularly when holding court, pint in one hand and briar pipe in the other, in the very corner of the Rose and Crown where his memorial stands today. Dick was a natural historian, a treasure trove of information and fascinating anecdotes about the Yorkshire Dales.

I met Dick only once, when I visited a fund-raising event at an old folks' home at Stalling Busk, a hamlet near Bainbridge, and we talked most of the afternoon away. Since then I have become acquainted with his married daughters, Signy and Denny, who live in Wensleydale. They tell one story about their father which gives some small indication of that unique talent to improve the quality of life of his pupils. When he taught at Shipley, near Bradford, one of them, a boy called Sutcliffe, was afflicted with a dreadful stammer. So one day Dick took him into an empty classroom and asked him to sing. The lad said it was impossible, but Dick gently persevered with him and eventually got his confidence. He began to sing. After that he hardly had any trace of a stammer. It just needed someone to take the time and interest to lead him out of his problem. His daughters also said that so many of his grateful scholars used to come and visit him in the holidays and after he retired that he was obliged to produce a booklet with information about Wensleydale to give them, which also contained advice about how to treat the countryside – being careful not to damage the dry stone walls, and so on. He would also arrange accommodation.

Barry Cockcroft knew him far better than I. He met him in the mid-sixties when he began to trawl the Yorkshire Dales for stories and characters to film and write about. Dick became his friend and mentor, and Barry spent many hours listening to Dick's fascinating tales of the Dales, including a vivid description of his own childhood and early life.

Dick was the second son of a farmer, which is very significant. Nobility and Dales farmers have one thing in common when it comes to

(*top*) Dick Chapman
demonstrates the art of
catching. . .
(*bottom*) . . . a succulent crayfish.

the matter of inheritance. The eldest son of a belted earl or baronet succeeds to the title and, usually, the entire estate that goes with it – stately home, Old Masters, the land, investments, everything. The same system traditionally applied to farming families in the Dales who owned the house and land they worked, only much further down the scale of course. So when the second son grew to manhood he usually had to leave home and seek his fortune elsewhere, more often than not going to a poorly paid job on a farm far away, while his elder brother became his own master, enjoying the real advantages and local esteem that went with the position. Dick Chapman may have trodden the same path so many second sons in the Dales did before him, had he not had the amazing luck to meet, in a place and at a time when education was not considered a priority, an improbable character with the same qualities Dick was to discover within himself in later life. Prior to that seminal event he spent an idyllic childhood in one of the most special places on this island, as he once described to Barry Cockcroft in his own words.

Signy and Denny, Dick's daughters, tell me about their father (*right – Hawes Church in the background*)

118

I was born on 24 March 1895, in Askrigg on the very day that the worst storm in living memory ended. It had started on Boxing Day 1894, and apparently only the winter of 1947 rivalled it.

My father, who was a farmer and butcher, used to go to Swaledale on Wednesdays with his horse and trap. But that winter he went with horse and sled, riding over the frozen snow which was so high that he could not find the road or the walls. Everything was totally obliterated. But the thaw came suddenly on the day I was born and everyone said that my appearance with bright red hair started it off.

When I was very young I can remember the old toll booth in Askrigg, where the farmers used to pay their market dues. The money was used for cobbling roads and putting in sewers. There was a prison underneath it, with a big heavy door with a grille in it, wooden seats and a bucket. I could recall the smell of that place for the rest of my life – rank, black, twist tobacco. When the local policeman arrested someone, usually a vagrant or a drunk, he would be put there for the night before being taken down to the sergeant at Leyburn. I'm afraid we boys used to shout rude things at the person inside, and we learned quite a lot of new swear words that way.

Before I went to school I had to milk the cows before breakfast and then milk them again when I came home. When I went to the old Yorbridge Grammar School, which was founded in 1601, I used to do my maths homework in my head as I milked. Milking soon becomes a subconscious action. The grammar school, by the way, only had eleven pupils, so everybody made the football team.

We had some remarkable animals on our farm. I had a dog, a mongrel collie called Boy, which I brought up from being a puppy. That dog – it knew what I was thinking. If I started off to bring the cows in, the dog knew without being told and it would go and round them up for me. Same with the sheep. And when I went swimming in the river it would go with me, stand on the side of the bank until I was ready and then dive in with me. It was a grand pal, that dog. I had two other pets, a lamb and a cow without horns. They would follow me everywhere, even when they grew up, and so would one of the hens. The cow had a habit of putting its head under my arm to pull sugar and biscuits out of my pocket with its tongue. People must have thought me an odd sight – a cow under my arm, a hen perched on my shoulder, Boy at my heels and a sheep jumping up at me like a dog!

My elder brother didn't approve of all this. Once, when he was coming through some thick snow, the sheep mistook him for me

In the corner of the Rose and Crown which will be forever his, Dick Chapman tells his cronies about the fish that got away.

and jumped at him. He was so surprised he fell backwards into a drift and couldn't get up, because he was carrying a back can full of milk. He was there a good five minutes before I found him, and when I pulled him out he said: 'This isn't a farm, it's a bloody menagerie!'

Then I met the man who was to make such a difference in my life. He was a kind of educational missionary called Theodore Grubb. It happened when I went down to Bainbridge one night to play football, and this man came to talk to me. I had seen him knocking about the village before. Apparently, he'd taught at an advanced school in the South and had been asked by the Rowntree Trust to try and promote further education among the farm lads in the Dales, going around the villages and holding classes. He had started running evening classes in Askrigg, teaching English and French, and he asked me if I would like to attend. I said I would try. In those days you could buy copies of Shakespeare's plays for a penny, and the first time I went he started reading *Twelfth Night*. Well, it sounded so fascinating that I asked if I might buy it. I took it home and carried it everywhere, reading it when I had a bit of spare time while working around the farm. I enjoyed it so much that I took a shilling to Mr Grubb and he got me twelve more plays. I read them in bed, sitting in the hedgerows, working on the farm, and they lasted me through to the end of winter. And I read the lot, every word.

Then Mr Grubb began producing *Twelfth Night* and lots of other plays, encouraging us to act in them. We even did plays by George Bernard Shaw – and it turned out that he was a personal friend of Shaw, and had a postcard written to him by the great man himself, which I was privileged to see later on.

I found I badly wanted to go back to school and learn more as a result of all this. So when my father came to me one day to tell me officially that my elder brother would be inheriting the farm, I told him I wanted to be a teacher. He agreed to help me and I began by doing two terms as a pupil teacher at Askrigg School. At seventeen I went to Northallerton Grammar School, which meant catching the seven o'clock train every morning. But it was a first-class school, with a lot of young, enthusiastic teachers not much older than myself. When I qualified to go to a Teacher Training College in Leeds I was surprised to find that I had read a deal more than any of the town lads. They even made me president of the union in my senior year.

In 1913 I had rheumatic fever. It was so bad that they thought I

An aerial view of Askrigg, Dick's birthplace.

could never walk again and I was reduced to hobbling around on sticks for months. But it probably saved my life because they wouldn't let me into the army on medical grounds. A lot of my generation were killed in the First World War. I did volunteer three times, and actually spent 24 hours in the Green Howards before they found me out.

I became a teacher in 1916, and went to a school in a pit village near Middlesbrough, although I was warned against going as it was a terribly rough place. But I liked the people very much and the experience affected my politics for life. They had a lot of accidents in the local mines, far more than they should have had. You always knew when something had happened because the sirens would go. I remember standing in the schoolyard after one incident, watching them bring a stretcher down. If the blanket was totally covering the miner he was dead, but this one was alive. I looked over and it was a boy I had been teaching only a few months before, and he was a grand lad. He had broken his spine.

Living in that village made me go left politically and I was elected as a Labour Councillor. The party even offered me a chance to stand for Parliament, but then I realized that if I won I would have to spend a lot of time in London. That was not an attractive proposition for a Dalesman like me.

I spent some years teaching in Shipley which taught me quite enough about living in a city, since it was so close to Bradford. But I never missed a chance to get back to Wensleydale. Before that, in 1918, I became headmaster at Askrigg School on a temporary basis. The man I stood in for had suffered a nervous breakdown. While I was there we had the first teachers' strike because the North Riding refused to apply the new Burnham Scale, although the government and the union had agreed to it. I was one of the leaders of the strike, and I can tell you we had a job persuading some of the old maiden ladies teaching in the village schools to come out with us. The strike went on until the Minister of Education told the North Riding Education Committee that if they didn't come into line, he would stop all educational grants, which would mean that everything would have to be paid out of rates.

Personally, I was only on strike for ten days, as headmasters had to give three months' notice against the teachers' one. And because of those ten missing days, my pension was reduced by five shillings (25p) a week.

But Dick Chapman had a glorious retirement. His new appointment as water bailiff only went a small part of the way to make up that five shillings a week, for his annual stipend was a mere £5. But it gave him the freedom of the local rivers, and he did not waste the opportunity. One of his special delights was to take privileged people to his secret river (confidentiality maintained to this day by everyone, for obvious reasons) where he would demonstrate how to catch unusual and succulent prey – freshwater crayfish. At their best they could be like dainty lobsters, and delicious to taste. The local otters obviously thought so too, because piles of empty shells would be found on the banks from time to time. At least, they once could – but who knows how the otters or the crayfish of Wensleydale are faring today as pollution increases everywhere?

Dick knew all about the crayfish, where they were, and how to catch them, since boyhood. Other rivers have crayfish, but almost invariably small, restricted in number, and inedible. Why these particular crustacea became superior, similar in size and flavour to those for sale at inflated prices in French restaurants, is a mystery to me. Legend suggests that they were introduced to that particular river by one of the Norman monks from a Cistercian abbey in the Dales, which has the ring of probability. He must have been missing the food of his native France!

Happily, no one has tried to catch the crayfish on a commercial basis, although it was once proposed. Many years ago J.B. Priestley arrived at Bainbridge to write an article for *Life* magazine, and was taken crayfishing by Dick, who afterwards received a letter from a firm of soup manufacturers offering one shilling a crayfish for as many as he could catch.

Dick had the skill to haul them out of the river at the rate of a bucketful an hour, but, being an ecologist to his fingertips, he turned them down flat. They were to be conserved, and taken out sparingly, for the enjoyment of locals and friends. Occasionally, they would be handed round the bar of the Rose and Crown where Dick, sitting in the corner he was to make his own for all time, and his fishing cronies would while away the winter hours around the fire, swapping stories about the giant trout that got away, and the record catches of the past.

11

Hornblowers and Metcalfes

*N*owhere in the North are old customs protected with such zeal as in Upper Wensleydale. Which is why, at nine o'clock every night between Holyroode and Shrovetide (that's 27 September to Ash Wednesday for the uninitiated) a sound very similar to the one an old cow makes when in distress issues mournfully from the village green of Bainbridge, and travels on the night air to bounce off the surrounding fells.

The Forest Horn has been blown at the same time for longer than anyone knows. But it's said records go back over 750 years. Neither is anyone certain why this habit was started in the first place, but there are two credible theories. Once Bainbridge was entirely surrounded by a thick forest – the place was created by verderers – and some believe it was blown to guide poor travellers trying to find their way through the trees in the dark. Others say that no one in their right mind would want strangers arriving on their doorstep in the middle of the night, and assert that it was either a curfew horn or a warning to the local monks who had grazing rights in the area that it was high time to get their cattle back across the river into the safety of the abbey that stood nearby.

Another theory, less disputed, is that the Forest Horn must be blown by a Metcalfe. And it has been said that only a Metcalfe can hit the top C on the instrument necessary to carry the sound a distance of over three miles. Since the Metcalfes proliferate to such an amazing extent in the Bainbridge area and electoral officers are driven to despair every election time, they have managed to hang on to the privilege, although it was momentarily threatened recently.

The most celebrated of recent Hornblowers was Jamie's Jack Metcalfe – most Metcalfes have double-barrelled forenames to assist identification. He blew it for 36 years, exactly the same time as his

Bainbridge.

father before him. The honoured position was also held by Jamie's Jack's grandfather, great-grandfather and so on in an unbroken chain which stretches away into the mists of time. Sadly, Jamie's Jack had no sons to hand on to, which created a crisis among the family. But he hung on until past the age of eighty, which meant that some of the next generation, his nephews, were getting past their prime. So the attention was focused on a youngster of tender years, his great-nephew, Alistair Metcalfe. It became a classic example of forward planning. Alistair tells the story.

I was just an infant of seven or eight when Great-Uncle started to teach me how to blow the horn in the hope I would succeed him. He had me practise on the old one at first, which is a cow horn and not used any more because it is supposed to be around eight hundred years old and a touch delicate. It was replaced in 1864 by a buffalo horn from South Africa, 85 centimetres long, presented to the village by a gentleman from Bishop Auckland. The old cow horn doesn't have a mouthpiece like its successor, so it took a bit of effort to get the right sound out of it. Then I moved up to the buffalo horn

(*This page*) (*top*) James Metcalfe, the father of Jamie's Jack, taken in 1920. (*bottom*) Jamie's Jack Metcalfe, Alistair's great uncle, taken in 1973.

(*Opposite*) (*left*) A youthful Hornblower – Alistair Metcalfe aged 11 in 1983. (*right*) Alistair Metcalfe, 1992.

and I had to work hard on that too. It was an education that lasted three years.

My great-uncle was a kind man, a good teacher, and a real character. He was often photographed and interviewed by newspapers and magazines and had a great answer, frequently quoted, whenever he was asked how far the sound carried:

Well, they do tell three miles. But I can't guarantee it, because I am always at this end!

Unofficially, I began to blow the Forest Horn on the green before my tenth birthday, under his supervision. It wasn't long after that, in 1981, that Great-Uncle died. He was eighty-three and still the official Hornblower. I was ten, and too young to be allowed to go to the funeral, although I wanted to. It was a well-attended ceremony, with the Forest Horn on display. He even used to joke about his own funeral. Our chapel steps have an awkward bend in them, so

he said they could carry him up, but he would get out of the coffin at the top and walk down by himself!

Then came the business of appointing the next Hornblower. And they put my name forward to the parish council, but they were a bit wary of giving the position to a ten-year-old.

Anyway, this debate about the successor spread over three months, and all during that time I was blowing the Forest Horn. That is what finally persuaded them to appoint me.

I have held the position for more than ten years now. Whenever I am away, and I am taking a Computer and Business Studies Degree at Huddersfield University, my grandfather deputizes. I get long holidays, and I am mostly home at weekends, as well. If Grandad has to stop for any reason then I would want it to be a Metcalfe to take his place. I have no brothers, so it would have to be one of my cousins.

We Metcalfes don't want any break in the tradition.

Nappa Hall, home of the man who fought the last private war in England.

130

And there are so many of them. Records show that they were paying taxes in Wensleydale in 1300, and one of them, James Metcalfe, made enormous sums of money dealing in booty while serving as quarter-master in the French campaign of 1415, which concluded with Agincourt and the immortal 'Once more into the breach dear friends, once more!' speech that Shakespeare put to the mouth of *Henry V.*

James built Nappa Hall and Raydale House in Wensleydale on his return, and the Metcalfes, who were clearly prodigiously prolific, virtually ruled the area for three centuries. James was Chief Forester of Wensleydale and when his descendant, Sir Christopher Metcalfe, was appointed High Sheriff of York in 1555, he rode into that city at the head of three hundred mounted men, every one a Metcalfe, every one on a white horse.

Now that must have been a sight to frighten anyone with plans to put the Metcalfes down. The family was always ready for a fight, going eagerly into any battle handy enough for them to reach. They even staged the last private war ever recorded in England.

It happened when Raydale House fell legally into the hands of the Robinson family, because of unpaid debts. A Sir Thomas Metcalfe was in residence at Nappa Hall at the time – he was known as the 'Black Knight of Nappa' – and he was clearly displeased by this turn of events. He rounded up sixty Metcalfes and their retainers and, armed with muskets, pikes, javelins and longbows laid siege to Raydale House for three days. Even the Metcalfe women turned up to shout encouragement to their warrior menfolk, and Lady Metcalfe is said to have tried to arrange by way of a bribe to have the place set on fire.

No, under the circumstances I wouldn't like to be the one to propose a person other than a Metcalfe to be the Hornblower of Bainbridge!

12

The £30,000 Tup

*T*he typical farmer in the higher reaches of the Yorkshire Dales is made of stern stuff. I suppose he has to be because of the
challenge nature flings at him most winters. Habitually a man of few
words, with features so weathered by the elements they appear to be
hewn from millstone grit, he meets the vagaries of the seasons with a
stoic resolve which rarely permits any outward show of emotion.
Whenever a crippling winter kills off a high proportion of his new-born
lambs, or falling farm prices wreck his annual budget, he invariably
grits his teeth, flings a curse or two up at the heavens and gets on with
the job.

Experiences of this kind down the generations have evolved a
special kind of farmer, purposeful, cautious – particularly with money –
and a person you trifle with at your peril. All underpinned by a fierce
pride – particularly in the quality of his stock. In Wensleydale and all
the higher dales, that means Swaledale sheep. There is nothing more
calculated to arouse the passions or loosen the purse strings of men
who find their living on the moorland fells than a quality Swaledale.
Particularly a fine tup, or ram, the male of the species, on which
depends the entire foundation of the flock and its future.

A prize tup can whip up such a storm of feeling among Dalesmen
that one which came to auction at Hawes market in recent times led to
dramatic scenes as the bidding went on and on, higher and higher.

Thirty thousand pounds! It was knocked down for £30,000, just one
four-legged, woolly beastie. A record – doubling the previous one –
for Hawes market, which, as you might imagine, still stands at the time
of writing. But I suppose another one will eventually come along and
bring everything boiling over again.

It was an outstanding event, still spoken of with awe wherever sheep
men gather, and the story behind it is fascinating. This tup was sold by

Hang on grimly! . . . me
and Glendale Jack Joe,
the £30,000 tup, with
Ronnie Metcalfe in the
background.

a man who is without peer in the matter of the selective breeding of Swaledale sheep. A Dalesman who habitually conjures up young tups that win prizes and persuade men who normally count every penny to throw financial caution to the winds. Yet he doesn't even have a farm of his own and – would you believe it – he is a Metcalfe.

Gordon Pratt, an authority on these matters, one of the leading auctioneers and valuers at Hawes market, and the man who did so well for me when he sold my possessions at Low Birk Hatt at public auction, describes him thus:

Ronnie Metcalfe is an artist at the job.

Now praise of any kind is a rare commodity in rural Yorkshire, so a statement like that from such an authoritative figure is very impressive. So I went to meet Mr Metcalfe and the £30,000 tup, and found them both on a farm near my old place in Teesdale. Buddle House near Ravenswood is run by father and son, Edward and Brian Lawson, who are also the owners of the tup. I discovered that Ronnie Metcalfe really has no roots, but has worked all his life as a journeyman shepherd moving from place to place. But he does have around a few sheep which go wherever he goes. He was born in 1929 in a village above Hawes called Camm, and worked with sheep from leaving school. This is the story he tells.

You see, I was always interested in sheep. Always, from being a little lad. I recall once a farmer asking me to learn his son about sheep and I said, like, I couldn't. He said, why, so I told him that his boy just wasn't interested enough. You have to give heart and soul to become a good sheep man. I always worked for a wage and didn't get any sheep of my own until the seventies. One day the farmer who employed me said he would buy me some sheep of my own choosing. So we went to a sale which included some I'd been keeping my eye on. But I waited until they'd been knocked down, and then went to the new owners and asked if they would sell a few of the older ones. My boss couldn't understand it, and asked me why I hadn't gone for some younger sheep instead of this lot. They had no teeth, and were just going to be killed. But I told him that I didn't want dear sheep, just these, and he had promised to buy whatever I wanted. They were only about £3 each, so he agreed. I had a bit of a problem with one man who had about twenty sheep, out of which I decided I wanted two. He insisted on knowing which two, so I told him that if I showed him he would know as much as me! I ended up telling him to keep them!

(*left*) Edward, the senior Lawson.
(*right*) Brian, his son.

I came away with eleven old sheep. You see, I knew them, every one, because I had worked on the farm where they had been bred. I used them to start my own flock, taking one or two to one tup and others to a second, all carefully chosen. Since then I have bred two champions – should have been five really – and a few reserve champions.

But it's not the judging by two men that matters. The thing which really counts is what people will bid for them when they get up to the sale room.

The £30,000 tup is called Glendale Jack Joe, named after two brothers who did me some favours. I always name my best tups after people who have been good to me. Jack and Joe Dixon bred the father which sired Glendale Jack Joe.

Ronnie is reticent about the total amount of money his tups have raised at auction over the years. He says he really doesn't want to add it up. He prefers to talk about the great pleasure he gets out of breeding tups that do well. But Gordon Pratt says a few of Ronnie's tups have fetched £15,000, and others regularly go at between £3,000 and £5,000. It can be good investment if you are lucky. There is a regular demand

(*top*) Swaledale tups come to market, Hawes, circa 1950.
(*bottom*) Tup sale in the top ring, Hawes market, same period.

(*top*) The young Gordon Pratt takes careful note as Jimmy Cloughton conducts the auction, 1959.

(*middle*) Gordon Pratt (*white coat*) wields the gavel, 1983.

(*bottom*) Proud new owner – Brian Lawson with Glendale Jack Joe on the day he bought him.

for new blood to avoid in-breeding, and a top tup with the right pedigree can make a lot of money for a big sheep breeder. Apparently, Glendale Jack Joe met all the exacting requirements of the Swaledale Sheep Breeders Association which was formed in 1920. Ronnie had nurtured him for eighteen months and he had grown into full, magnificent manhood, and was ready to sell. Ronnie says he knew the tup was something special from the very day he was born.

Brian Lawson had prior knowledge of Glendale Jack Joe because of previous dealings with Ronnie. He had bought a tup from him in previous years which had come on very well, particularly on the female side. It is essential for a big sheep farm to produce good draught ewes, which will raise good money at auction from farmers who need to change a bloodline. The Lawsons have 2,000 acres of fell land, a very hard place exposed to all weathers, so they also need sheep with the strength and stamina to withstand the elements.

The first thing you must look for when you go to market for a tup is a beast which is not too closely related to the stock you already have. And one of the problems with Ronnie is that he has had so much success down the years that it's difficult to avoid his strain, particularly with ewes.

But Glendale Jack Joe was different, unrelated to the Lawsons flock. And he had proven stamina, well able to cope with the extreme conditions on their fell. Ronnie told Brian about him before the auction. He inspected it, and quickly concluded it was just what he wanted. Then he told Edward, his father, who took one look at the tup just before it went into the ring and came to the same conclusion. The decision was made. And when Glendale Jack Joe was released into the middle at Hawes Auction Mart the atmosphere was electric. Several other top breeders had set their hearts on owning him.

The senior Lawson recalled the event.

The bidding went very fast because there were two syndicates against us, who meant to share the tup. But we were on our own. Ronnie was there, and when it got to £20,000 I saw his knees starting to wobble a bit. So did mine! You wondered when it would stop, but you had to keep going. The bids came down from a thousand to five hundred pounds a time. It got to £30,000, and that was our limit. Another £500 . . . but it stuck at £30,000. So it was ours. There was a lot of publicity which did us some good in one way, but not in another, as the tax man became interested. But Jack Joe went on to win the Tan Hill Show, and then the Great Yorkshire Show, so he became very fashionable. Other breeders regularly turn up wanting to buy one of his sons. We have two thousand sheep and we have put him to a hundred ewes on each of the five seasons we've had him. The average yield, since some ewes have twins, is upwards of 140 lambs. That's not bad at all. He has also sired champions and reserve champions. You can tell his offspring – they are all alert and able to withstand the snowstorms when they come. Mettled up, we call them. Jack Joe himself used to be the very devil to catch until he had a bit of an accident. He jumped a metal-framed door with a rough edge and damaged ligaments in one of his front legs. It was a bad moment for us because it was only about a fortnight before he was due to be moved to the ewes and his leg was a real mess. We kept hold of him until a lady vet came, and she was very good – didn't give him a full anaesthetic, just gave him a local and stitched him up where he stood. She put a plaster cast and a bandage on it. She told us that we couldn't expect to be able to use him to serve the ewes until the next year. But as soon as we let him go he was off, racing along on his wooden leg, and he covered more than a hundred of his ladies. We changed his bandage every two days and he finished up with scarcely a limp. But we had another do after that, which was much worse. One day we went into the field and he was laid down. He didn't get up until we walked across and then it became clear what was up. His back leg had gone. A dog did it – apparently some people saw it in the field, and there were other tell-tale signs. The damage was X-rayed and showed that a little bone had been broken in the leg. It was plastered up again but now he's riddled with arthritis. It wouldn't have mattered so much if it had been a front leg again but a tup needs his back legs for support when he's about his work. Normally, a good tup will last between ten and twelve years, but we will just have to see how Jack Joe goes on. It might be interesting to see what can be done with all the new veterinary techniques. I know of a dog with a leg smashed up from being run over with a tractor, which was taken to the vet at Leyburn. He put it to sleep, slit its back leg full length, took a bone or two out and put a steel pin in. Six or eight weeks later you couldn't tell it had been hurt, and it worked the sheep as good as ever. Maybe we could do the same for Glendale Jack Joe.

Anyway, it's possible to take semen from him to store. They say it will be good in the deep freeze for fifteen years, so he can be siring lambs long after he is dead. That will be very handy because it is good to have three or four crosses out before you come back with the same tup, so it will be there for my grandson, Matthew, to use when he takes over.

A double dynasty! First Glendale Jack Joe and his children, then the Lawsons. Father Edward is in his seventies, son Brian in his late forties, and grandson Matthew just gone twenty. Meanwhile, Ronnie Metcalfe has been allowed by the Lawsons to take some of his own ewes each year to Jack Joe, and says he has had at least three of his sons every time. He refuses to be drawn on whether he has another potential champion amongst them, but the Lawsons reckon he's got one up his sleeve somewhere. And they are clearly very happy with their investment in Glendale Jack Joe, despite the inflated price. Ronnie himself still lives his nomadic life on the fells, and freely admits that he had a spot of trouble with the Inland Revenue over the large sums his unique skill yielded. He says he wasn't trying to avoid paying, just got into a muddle because he didn't understand the system. Anyway, he had to pay a fine plus interest on the money he owed, so that knocked a big hole in his savings.

Ronnie is in his sixties now, and his reputation will probably last for as long as the Swaledale breed remains the dominant one along the higher fells. Gordon Pratt, who has been valuing and auctioning cattle and sheep since the 1950s, says the Swaledale evolved from the Scottish Blackface – the origin of most Dales livestock can be traced

Swaledale sheep on the move on Stonesdale Moor, near Tan Hill.

back across the border – and the breeders gradually produced a sheep that could stand the climate and had the strength to travel great distances to find food, right to the wildest areas which place them at risk if a sudden snowstorm comes. But Swaledales are capable of surviving up to two weeks buried under six feet of snow, as long as they have an air hole. That also gives the dogs a chance to sniff them out after the storm abates, and many a hundred have been dug out, a bit thinner and very hungry but otherwise none the worse for their experience. According to Mr Pratt, who followed his grandfather to Hawes Auction Mart and is an authority, you won't find many Swaledales on the other side of Kendal and around Cumbria, because they don't suit the ground there. The grazing is different, apparently. Over there they mainly have a breed called the Kendal Rough, which has a different coat, coarser and straighter than the Swaledale which has curly wool. Uncle liked the Swaledale breed and we once had fifty or sixty at Low Birk Hatt, but our neighbour at High Birk Hatt, John Britton, preferred the Kendal Rough. They were the quieter kind. But we only had Swaledale ewes which we used to cross with what we called a mug tup, a breed without horns which were once known as Wensleydales and then called Teeswaters. You had to be very careful to keep tups apart when the season started because they would fight, particularly mug tups and Swaledales, because the Swaledales had the advantage of horns. Swaledales are well known to be a particularly lively breed and no respecters of boundaries, and even though we crossbred, we still had problems trying to keep them on our land. You see, Low Birk Hatt was what they called an inside farm as opposed to a moor farm. If you want to keep Swaledales you need the grazing rights to a good stretch of moorland so they can wander. We had no such rights.

Keeping sheep can be a risky business. No matter how good and careful you are there are always tragedies. We had a few at Low Birk Hatt. I recall we lost one good tup and had to borrow a replacement from a neighbour. So I think the Lawsons were very brave to pay £30,000 for one tup, that could have died the very next day.

13

Shepherds, Sheepdogs . . .
and Katy Cropper

*L*ike the prize Swaledales they care for, shepherds
are a particular breed. They need the energy of mountain goats to
cover the miles of rough ground, moving quickly up and down the
highest fells to keep pace with the flocks in their charge. Probably the
only creature physically fitter than the average Dales shepherd is his
dog. And shepherds all seem to share the same characteristics – thin,
wiry frames, faces like antique leather and a marked disinclination to
indulge in idle conversation. With one notable exception.

Katy Cropper.

She is, without doubt, the most unusual personality you will find
along the upper reaches of Wensleydale. Pretty as a picture with long
dark hair and as friendly and chatty as they come, she is a shepher-
dess – and the only woman, up to now, ever to win the BBC's *One Man
and His Dog* competition. That would be remarkable enough if Katy
had been reared to life on the fells, the daughter of a Dales farmer. But
her background is about as far removed from that as is possible.

The daughter of a headmaster, she was privately educated, owned a
pony, went to art college and seemed all set for a different and much
more comfortable career than the one she leads now. But everything
changed dramatically one day when she watched a sheepdog trial in
Anglesey. All she wanted to do from that moment on was to work with
sheepdogs. She went to the Agricultural Training Board and they
arranged for her to be taught. She lived for two years in a caravan
looking after a field full of sheep, and says she never went out and
socialized throughout this period of training. Her family didn't like it –
she says they almost disowned her – and everyone declared she
would never make it. But this young lady has determination and, fortu-

Katy Cropper and
friends.

nately for her, the necessary strength and stamina to cope with the
work. The record she set for running the mile at school has only recently been broken – and she is now turned thirty.

She started competing with a dog called Sykes, and she was ambi-
tious enough to suggest to a man connected with the *One Man and His
Dog* show that she should be considered for a place on the programme. He agreed to watch her perform at a sheepdog trials and she
cheerfully admits it was a disaster. She couldn't whistle properly,
totally lost her confidence and the sheep ended up in the beer tent!

But Katy persisted, found a tutor who taught her how to whistle and
how to impose her authority on dog and sheep. She ended up beating
him at trials, the pupil overcoming the master. And she did it with a
three-legged sheepdog!

The story of Lad is really heart-warming. He was found hanging up on a fence by his back leg, which he had obviously tried to jump, and he had been there so long all his ligaments were ripped to shreds. Under normal circumstances Lad would have been put down, but Katy pleaded for his life, had the ruined leg removed, and kept him as a pet – at first. Then one day while walking him over the fells they came across some sheep and she decided to try him out. He was off like a shot, rounding them up. So she began to enter him for trials. At first he didn't do well, but he eventually improved and at one event on a big steep hillside near Preston he beat a lot of good competition from nearly ninety dogs – and the judge didn't even realize he only had three legs. Katy says she learned more from that dog than from any human tutor because he had a natural feel for sheep. Apparently, he even qualified for the English National Championships, but the organizers banned him because he had a leg missing.

Katy has trained many dogs since those early days, worked on a sheep farm in Norfolk looking after large number of lambs and eventually moved into Wensleydale, where she now lives in a cottage at Sedbusk, just above Hawes. In 1990, after her prowess had been noted in the national press she was invited to compete in *One Man and His Dog*, with a dog called Trim, and won it.

Showtime . . . Katy Cropper and an appreciative audience.

I met both Trim and Lad when I visited Katy at her cottage. It is true – most people would never notice that Lad is missing a back leg. Katy is now a celebrity. She has appeared on the *Wogan* show with Lad and published a book about her life and experiences. She has also developed a novelty demonstration which has become very popular at agricultural shows. It includes a black sheep called Fergie which thinks it's a dog, and a flock of ducks which are driven through gates and on to a slide into a pool. All that, plus a three-legged sheepdog. The crowds love it.

Lad is getting up in years now, and dog and mistress are clearly very much attached to each other. He followed her about everywhere. And Trim was lovely too. He even came and offered his paw to me. I tried to train sheepdogs in a much more modest way when I was younger, just to get them to do simple jobs like taking the cows up into the top pastures. Every stock farm needs dogs, but I never seemed to find the patience or ability to train one properly. Maybe I wasn't hard enough to apply the necessary discipline.

Uncle would train them, and I recall we once had a lovely working dog called Fly which he got from good breeding stock. She was quite an unusual dog, very bonny with a nice personality and a smooth blue-and-grey coat. During the 1940s Uncle and I went on a few cattle drives with Fly, taking the cattle to the auction market at Middleton-in-Teesdale. It was quite a distance, maybe six or seven miles, going first of all over the tops and then down along the road. It meant an overnight stop along the way, usually with my cousin Norman and his wife Lizzie at Mickleton. The cattle would spend the night on his land.

It wasn't a journey that I liked, because I used to get into upsets worrying about the things that could go wrong, particularly when the cattle were among traffic. Uncle used to tell me to keep back and watch the rear. I think he rather enjoyed the occasion, but I was always on pins. There were regular incidents, with cattle jumping over gates and the like, particularly when we were taking neighbours' cattle to market. Rather like people, cattle can be nervous with strangers. They tend to hang on to the ones they are used to being with and sometimes there would be arguments. In my experience, sheep were better to drive than cattle.

Once we had got them to market I would retreat to Norman's place. Lizzie and I would talk and read books while Uncle took care of the business side of things. One summer Norman bought a cow from us and Uncle and I walked it over. Uncle was able to stop the night, but for some reason I had to get back. It was a beautiful, warm, moonlit night, so after supper I set off over the moors on my own across the tops and down into Baldersdale. I really enjoyed it. Ah, those were the days!

I did that walk on my own on a previous occasion, but in less happy circumstances. On one drive Fly was very badly kicked by one of the cattle, and when we arrived at Mickleton it was obvious she wasn't fit to work. The next day Uncle agreed to let me take her home. I don't know how on earth he managed to complete the journey to market without a dog.

Poor Fly, she made very painful progress back to Low Birk Hatt. In the end I had to pick her up and carry her home.

Me with Katy, Lad and Trim, and Fergie, the black sheep that thinks it's a dog.

146

14

The Royal Rabbits of Carperby

*R*abbits are part of the fabric of the Yorkshire Dales. They are everywhere, part pest but also something very useful for the pot. I am generally not too keen on eating rabbit myself, but I remember in the old days Mrs Fawcett of West Birk Hatt in Baldersdale would bring us a rabbit pie with a good thick crust bigger than the dish, and that was a treat. But rabbits do eat a lot and can damage your land. Occasionally, they would strip whole parts of my pastures, leaving nothing for the beasties.

Now in size, shape and colouring one rabbit is very much like another. But in one part of the Dales there once flourished a very special rabbit. A royal rabbit, you could say. They were black when babies and then turned to a very attractive silver-grey, and they were unique to an 80-acre piece of land at Carperby, a village in Wensleydale between Leyburn and Aysgarth. The pelts were highly prized, and the Russian royal family used to buy them to trim their ceremonial clothes. It is said that one tsar of Russia had a helmet made of this fur, and the ill-fated Tsar Nicholas was presented with a coat entirely lined with pelts from Carperby rabbits.

They were important and valuable enough to justify having a house built alongside the warren – still called Warren House to this day – and paying wages to a gamekeeper to look after them. No one knows how the Carperby breed began, but local legend says Sir Walter Raleigh introduced them. For several generations the land, house and rabbits belonged to the Vyners, a wealthy and well-connected family based in Ripon, who also owned Nappa Hall, once the seat of the mighty Metcalfe family, and lots of other land and farms in the surrounding Dales. But both the Vyners and the rabbits have gone and, but for the fact that the land is still referred to as The Warren and the adjoining house the same, the memory of the royal rabbits of Carperby would be

(*top*) Inspecting the
remains of the Royal
Warren, with Roland
Raw, Walter Dunsdale
and Keith Dinsdale
(Walter's grandson).

(*bottom*) The Dinsdales
show me their sole
surviving pelt.

almost obliterated. As far as I know only one silver-grey pelt survives in the village, and that belongs to the descendants of a man who once worked for the Vyners as their rabbit keeper. The same local family now owns both land and house. I went to meet and talk to them and was shown the pelt, which is a carefully cherished memento, as you might imagine. It is owned by Mr and Mrs Walter Dinsdale, who live in a beautiful old house in Carperby, opposite The Wheatsheaf public house which has been featured in the *All Creatures Great and Small* television series as the place where the young James Herriot and his bride spent their honeymoon. The elder of the family is Roland Raw, Walter's uncle, who is well into his eighties now, and he has vivid memories of the days when the rabbits flourished.

My grandfather, James Storey, was employed by the Vyners to look after the rabbits and lived in Warren House. He often told the story of the coat made for Tsar Nicholas which I think he said was presented by the Vyner family, which indicates they must have had a lot of influence in high places. Grandad had to guard against poachers, watching out particularly at night for flashlights in the warren. It was like a rabbit city, spreading over the 80 acres with triple-decker runs in some of the bigger mounds. We could never work out just how many rabbits there were but it must have been more than a thousand. They were never easy to catch, and a complicated set of traps were built into the ground, so deep that when I was a lad one came up to my chin when I stood in it. They were quite ingenious, with lead-weighted doors, and we would try and drive the rabbits in when they came out to feed in the evenings. They had to be taken alive for shipping out to customers. A game dealer in Aysgarth called Frank Graham was the agent, and Grandfather had to send off the rabbits, six at a time, in boxes with holes bored in for ventilation. A turnip was placed in every box for nourishment – a field was set aside for growing the turnips – and they would go on the seven o'clock train under the direction of Mr Graham. He used to be very fussy, making sure the boxes were nailed up properly, and the string to tie them to the carriage seats was good and strong and properly knotted.

It's a mystery, not only how the rabbits came to Carperby, but also how they seemed to be able to flourish here and nowhere else. I heard that many attempts were made to set up warrens in places as far away as Scotland, Holland and Belgium. But they never succeeded. I know from my late brother, Robert James Raw, who took over the job from my grandfather, that there were accusations from

A very old photograph of grandfather James Storey, holding a Royal rabbit.

some frustrated clients that they must be sending old bucks and does past their breeding span! Thousands were packed off by train over the years but I don't think anyone in the village, not even my grandfather or my brother, ever found out how much they fetched. That was a confidential matter between Frank Graham and the Vyners.

They were very particular rabbits and didn't like strangers. If a hare managed to jump into the warren it wouldn't survive long. I think they must have chased intruders to their death, because we would just find a dead body with bits of fur scattered around.

Rabbits can be quite vicious, and we often saw them rearing up and fighting. The warren was enclosed, of course, and when the railway was built around 1890 it took about ten acres from the southern side. I understand the Vyners gave the railway company the land on condition they built a wall 8 foot high to keep the rabbits in. And I recall when I was a small boy seeing workmen come to erect a wire fence, on the south side again, because the Vyners planned to keep the rabbits off that bit and run racehorses there. But the First World War came along, the racing industry collapsed, and no horses ever appeared. Just as well, as it happened, because it wasn't a good place. Apart from being stony, it was covered with bracken which turned out to be poisonous. We found that out when we began to run cattle on the land when it became ours and lost a young heifer. There was no spray invented to kill off the bracken in those days, so we had to cut them back and pull the roots out by hand. Some shoots had come back and the vet who came to look at the heifer said it had been poisoned by eating them. Anyway, we bought a tractor in 1948, and on the advice of the vet we ploughed the land up, reseeded it and killed off the bracken that way. The bracken didn't appear to poison the rabbits though, but by that time it didn't matter so much. Sometime during the 1920s their value fell overnight. That was when they developed a technique to dye the fur of ordinary brown rabbits any colour.

The Vyners sold Warren House and the land to my brother and gave my grandfather a pension. Eventually, the silver-greys were only worth as much as any other rabbit. Just good for the pot. We sold them to game dealers and because there were so many around our land we did a good trade, particularly during the Second World War when meat was short, and during the Depression in the thirties. One dealer used to come twice a week from Stockton and collect all the way up the Dales. He said the miners in his area used to take as many as they could get when food rationing was in force. For youngsters like Walter, my nephew, it was an easy way of making a bit of extra money. There was a standing agreement with the local farmers. They would let the lads on to their land with their ferrets and snares on condition that half the cash raised was handed over.

It didn't matter to the dealer whether the rabbits were brown or silver-grey. And he wanted them dead, which made life a lot easier. The best price was around Christmas when they could go up to a pound a pair. On a good day you could catch ten pair, but there was a lot of competition – plenty of other local lads out catching rabbits to put a shilling or two in their pockets.

Then came two disasters. The first was the winter of 1947, a terrible time when the storm lasted for weeks and all the roads were blocked. It's a wonder any wildlife survived at all. The rabbits came down from the hills and ran in the village street, but they were no good to eat. Starving they were, just skin and bone. Even the grouse came off the moors and would perch hopefully in the trees and on the tops of the walls when we were foddering the cattle.

Even worse was to follow in the 1950s. Myxomatosis. How this disease spread everywhere we never knew. It started down the dale and advanced rapidly. It was painful to watch those poor rabbits. Their heads would swell up and scabs covered their eyes. They scarcely had the strength to crawl, never mind run. We tried keeping the brown ones away, killing and burying them right away, but it spread to the silver-greys.

It was a long time before we saw any kind of rabbit in this dale after myxomatosis. Lots of local kids were born and lived several years before they knew what one looked like, except for pictures. Gradually, a few began to pop up again, so some must have either recovered or been immune. Now, of course, they are back in full strength.

But none of the silver-grey rabbits have ever been seen again.

I have a grandson who says he's seen some black rabbits but their fur never changed into silver-grey. Perhaps they may be lurking around somewhere.

I hope so. I would be glad to see them back.

15

Bolton Castle and the Legend of the Scottish Queen

*B*olton Castle stands like a grim sentinel, perched four square and rising to a hundred feet on a hillside above the main road leading into Upper Wensleydale. It is not exactly a beautiful building, since it appears to have been constructed for utilitarian and defensive purposes rather than to please the eye. Yet it probably has more romantic associations than any other great house in the western Dales.

It was built in the fourteenth century by Sir Richard Scrope, the first Baron Scrope of Bolton, and twice the Chancellor of England. A remarkable Dales family, the Scropes. Several held high office – one was the Archbishop of York who officiated at the coronation of Henry IV – and they were eager to participate in any military campaign within reach. But they had a habit of finishing on the losing side of plots and rebellions against the crown, and many a Scrope head rolled from the executioner's block, even the Archbishop's. William Shakespeare seized upon this unfortunate family propensity (altering the name slightly to Scroop) and wrote them into *Henry V* and *Richard II*, which gave rise to the expression 'hanging a Scroop'. The character executed for treason in *Henry V* was Lord Henry Scroop of Masham.

All colourful enough, but another personality indelibly associated with Bolton Castle transcends them all. Mary, Queen of Scots. When she was defeated in battle in 1568 and fled to England, she asked for protection from Queen Elizabeth I – a dubious move as it turned out. Although Elizabeth, her cousin twice removed but with the same red hair, was obliged to treat her with the courtesy due to her rank, she placed restrictions upon her movements, and Bolton Castle was an ideal place to keep her since it was remote, and communications with the mainstream of life rather tenuous. She arrived on 15 July 1568, with many retainers, over fifty horses and several cartloads of belongings. She stayed over half a year, as her enemies attempted to bring her to trial for the alleged murder of her husband, Lord Darnley, and in that time one of the most romantic legends in the vivid history of the Dales was born: Mary's attempted escape to Scotland. The story goes that she went out hunting one day in the forest which covered Wensleydale in the fifteenth century. Since hunting was a regular activity for Mary it wouldn't arouse the suspicions of the Queen's men, as long as she came back within the expected time limit. She did return as normal, but slipped away again quietly, apparently bribing one of the guards to allow her to pass, saying she had lost a ring and keenly wished to find it.

It was some time before the alarm was raised and a pursuit organized. But Mary was unlucky. It seems that a piece of the shawl she wore was torn off on a thornbush on a ridge near Leyburn, the Queen's men spotted it hanging there and recognized it. She had made about six miles, heading north and east in the general direction of the Scottish border before they captured her. To this day, the point where the give-away piece of material was found is known as Shawl Way. I hear that some years ago there was even a pole bearing a notice marking the place where she was caught. Afterwards, Mary was moved south to Tutbury, thus placing more distance between her and potential support from Scotland.

That tale is challenged by one man who should know, the son and heir of Lord Bolton, who personally runs the castle today. The Honourable Harry Orde-Powlett is a direct descendant in a rather unusual way of the Scrope family, and he devotes much of his time now to the restoration of the building. He gave me a personally guided tour of the castle, and I found him to be such a pleasant young man. I must confess I thought that being an aristocrat he might be a bit stiff and formal, and I did wonder before we met what I would find to say to him. But he was perfectly charming and hospitable and I really liked him. He helped to carry the equipment for the photographic session, and made and fetched coffee for us. We had a discussion about the art of walling, one of my regular summer occupations at Low Birk Hatt when the winter damage to the dry stone walls had to be put right. It turned out that Mr Orde-Powlett doesn't just give orders to workmen, he buckles down and gets his hands dirty. I inspected a stretch of wall he had built and I have to admit he makes a better job of it than I used to. He had all the proper stones facing outwards and manages to get them firmly set. It

(*top*) A man and his castle – the Hon. Harry Orde-Powlett.

(*bottom*) Examining a portrait of Bolton Castle's most famous resident.

was an absorbing visit to a place well worth seeing, and Mr Orde-Powlett was a fund of information about the place and its history, including the legend of Mary's escape bid.

It's a nice story, but I've been down to the Public Records and read through all the numerous letters concerning Mary, Queen of Scots, and not one of them mentions an actual escape. The word 'escape' is used in three letters, though – one from Sir Francis Knollys, appointed with Lord Scrope to guard Mary, saying, 'it would be easy for the Scottish Queen to escape, her servants might let her out of the window on a rope'. In another, written only a couple of weeks later, the same man says, 'the Scottish Queen is hunting daily, her people are with her and since they outnumber the lord's troops it would be easy for them to carry her away and effect an escape'. It's interesting to note that she was always referred to in the letters as 'the Scottish Queen'. The third and most interesting letter was written by Mary's stepbrother, the Earl of Moray, supposedly outlining plans to set her free.

But I suspect the originals were read and deciphered by someone from the Victorian era who was unable to translate them properly, but managed to see the word escape where it may really have meant something quite different. It was the letter about lowering Mary out of the window on a rope that probably created the legend. Then there is the business of the Shawl Way. In the language of the sixteenth century that word also has a geographical meaning, which slightly knocks down that theory.

Anyway, because of who she was, Mary posed a threat to the crown whether she wanted to or not. It took another eighteen years after she left Bolton Castle before they parted her head from her shoulders, for supposedly being involved in a plot against Elizabeth.

The Scrope family went on in their usual turbulent way. Twice we were at loggerheads with Henry IV, then part of a plot against Henry V, but gave shelter to Henry VI when he fled south after losing the battle of Hexham in 1464. Lord John Scrope looked after him well for a few days and was presented with a nice gift by the king as he left. But John almost certainly turned him in, because the Earl of Warwick – Warwick the Kingmaker – was waiting for him just down the road. He went straight to the Tower and inevitable death on the orders of Edward IV, and Scrope was given two important titles, both of which carried a pecuniary reward. He got it wrong next time by siding with Warwick when he rebelled against

A curlew's eye view of Bolton Castle.

Edward, but was pardoned. His luck held through two more mis-calculated mutinies against the throne, being pardoned again, but I think he was fined on the last occasion and ordered to live within 22 miles of London. Why 22 miles, I have no idea. Another Scrope became the Earl of Wiltshire but lost his head without the benefit of a trial when his great friend, Richard II, was being deposed.

I am related to the Scropes by marriage. Indeed, I like to tell the Americans who come to visit Bolton Castle that I am descended from a long line of bastards! The last Lord Scrope, Emmanuel, had two families. One legitimate by a wife who lived in Nottingham-shire, and another illegitimate by his housekeeper at Bolton Castle, called Martha James. All his legitimate children died in infancy so the property went to his son by Martha, who defended the castle on the side of the King in the Civil War. He died a year later in 1646 of the plague, so the estate was divided between his three sisters. Mary Scrope got the property up here and was legitimized by Act of Parliament. She married one of my Powlett ancestors. Their eldest son married an illegitimate daughter of the Duke of Monmouth, himself the illegitimate son of Charles II. After the Monmouth rebellion they decided they would change from Catholic to Protestant, and for that they were created the Dukes of Bolton. There were six dukes altogether before they ran out of legitimate children again, but the last duke had an illegitimate daughter who married a politician called Orde. He was a member of William Pitt's cabinet and was made the first Lord Bolton. I am his direct descendant, and my father is the present Lord Bolton.

The dukes were entertaining people. The first was supposed to be afraid of opening his mouth because he thought evil spirits would enter his body. He refused to go out in daylight, hunted his hounds at night, and had the most amazingly debauched banquets. He was supposed to have sold his soul to the devil, and according to legend was buried alive in an upright stone coffin in a vault below Wensley-dale Church. A Victorian book says that the coffin was left ajar and one arm hung out. His wife is in a similar coffin next to him. Her heart had a separate burial and is said to be in a little lead casket which sits on top of the coffin. I don't think anyone has been in that vault for sixty or seventy years.

The third duke had a mistress called Lavinia Fenton who played Polly Peachum in an 18th-century production of *The Beggar's Opera*. He couldn't stand the sound of her voice, which could reach a fair distance, so he built a tower on the other side of the valley for her to sing in.

None of my family lived in Bolton Castle after the restoration of Charles II. We built a more modern place in 1678 down the road, called Bolton Hall. The castle had a bad time during the Civil War and it was ordered by Cromwell's parliament to be dismantled and made untenable in 1674. But one of the conditions of the surrender following the siege said that Scrope's mother and sister could stay. I think they grumbled like mad when the breakers came to knock it down, so one end was left intact.

But they probably stripped off the lead and caved in the roof timbers on the other bit, and the weather did the rest. The castle was used as a farmhouse between the end of the seventeenth century and the beginning of the nineteenth. It was never totally neglected, and we have found bits of work done in the eighteenth and nineteenth centuries. A lot of money was spent just before the First World War, and again just afterwards. After I left Eton, I worked on the land, on a stud farm in Australia, came back to farm and did quite a lot of racing over jumps. I was always light enough and won a few races, but I wasn't a very successful farmer – in fact I was doing the opposite of making money – so I decided to find something else to do. I looked over the castle and thought it had potential. Part of it was then being used as a restaurant but the remainder was rather neglected, so I initially rented it from my father.

Basically, we are making the structure sound. I don't suppose the work will ever stop. In 1991 we spent £720,000, grant aided. Now I am doing it myself with three stonemasons. I'm not much good but I do it. I am the Master of the West of Yore Hunt and ride to hounds twice a week during the season, but the rest of the time you will find me here – de-vegetating the wall tops so they can be fixed, for instance. With a bit of luck the income from the visitors will exceed the outgoings in around three years' time.

Some strange things have occurred during the restoration. I'm not saying there are ghosts, but inexplicable happenings seem to be regular almost every time a group stays here. One night we had a dinner party for an historical re-enactment society who were wearing medieval dress. The floodlighting was on and they clearly saw two people talking on top of the tower. They thought it was two of their own group, so went to see what was going on. The only way up was through a door which was securely bolted. They opened it and climbed up.

But – there was nobody there.

16

The Postmaster with a Sixteen-pound Hammer

With Roland Parker
outside the prettiest Post
Office in the Dales.

Nestling in the shadow of Bolton Castle is a weatherbeaten old cottage, bedecked with an array of fruit trees and flowering plants, which would gladden the heart of any postcard publisher. It is, in fact, the village sub-post office, and I cannot imagine a prettier outpost of the GPO exists anywhere in the Yorkshire Dales. And when you go through its door you step back in time, because I daresay it hasn't changed perceptibly for at least a couple of generations.

Castle Bolton sub-post office is presided over by a true character, who has lived and worked in and around the village for over seventy years. Roland Parker can recall the time when more than a hundred people inhabited Castle Bolton. Now there are just a handful. By the way, I find it a trifle odd that the village is called Castle Bolton, so Bolton Castle is, I suppose, the principal residence of Castle Bolton.

Roland's home is more pleasing to the eye than the castle, which is a stern and forbidding place. Growing along Roland's walls is an apple tree reputed to be two hundred years old, and it still yields him enough fruit to keep him going all through the winter and right up to Easter. Two other apple trees died, presumably of old age, but Roland replaced them many years ago with a plum tree which is also a generous fruiter. All set off by a clump of lovely honeysuckle thriving on the same wall.

Roland is not a Dalesman born and bred, but no one would ever know. He was born in Nelson, Lancashire, in 1915 and came to Castle Bolton when he was six. His father was a quarryman, one of a group hired to open up a limestone quarry, which flourished for a while on the hill a mile above the village. Roland is a classic example of a breed

of man who had to strain every sinew in his body to make a living. Something scarcely imaginable these days. Even his schooling required a goodly measure of physical effort.

Yes, I walked 3½ miles up and down the hills, twice a day to go to school in Wensley. There were no such things as buses in those days, and only people like doctors and parsons could afford push-bikes. When I was fourteen I went to quarry, working with a 16 lb hammer.

From the Parker family album . . . Roland at the ages of seven, eleven and with his bride to be, Mary.

Newlywed Mrs Mary Parker inspects Roland's patch at the limestone quarry.

It was piece work – we were paid ninepence, old pence mind, for every ton of limestone we brought out. Ten tons a day meant you were doing well. But you had to pay for your own explosives, and the rock drilling. It was sixpence a foot, knocked out of your wages each week, for drilling into your space. The stone came out in great big sections and you had to break them down into lumps of 27 lbs in weight, then load them into a bogie, two tons at a time. My father was working at the same job and wages used to average at around 35 or 36 shillings a week. If you could make £2, you were doing well. It may have been hard work, but it was a sight better paid than other jobs around here, if you could land one. By the time I got into my teens I was a strong lad, earning more than my dad. The quarry closed down for a while when the company running it went bank-rupt, so the two of us got work helping to build a new army camp near Leyburn, digging the drains, putting in the plumbing, building cookhouses – anything that required a bit of muscle. Then the quarry reopened. So I went back to breaking rocks, and I did that job on and off for various quarries around here until 1947, when I got fed up after the big storm that winter and found work in a flour mill in Aysgarth. I wasn't allowed to go into the Forces during the war because quarrying was classed as essential work, but I joined the Territorials, did the training and spent weekends in uniform with the Home Guard. Every Wednesday was my turn, along with two others, to spend the night from 11 p.m. until 6 a.m. on the hill

Portrait of Roland Parker, 1992.

overlooking Castle Bolton watching out for enemy parachutists and the like!

I got married in 1937 – my wife was a Burnley lass – and went to live about three miles from the village in Preston-under-Scar. I worked for a spell as a labourer at Catterick Camp and managed to afford a pushbike, working until 7 o'clock every night and cycling ten miles back home against the west wind in all weathers. It would be ten at night before I could sit down to read the paper. Then we came back to the family home in the village and reared two daughters, Joan and Carole.

The opportunity to start a post office happened in 1948, when a parish meeting decided to ask the Head Postmaster at Northallerton if the village could have one of its own. Up to then we had to go down to Redmire for our stamps. We used to say it was a mile down to Redmire and two miles back because of the hill! My wife was running a little shop out of the house, selling groceries and bits of everything, which my mother had started back in 1926, so we were given the go ahead for this sub-post office.

The village has always been a tourist attraction because of the castle. It was open to the public when we arrived here. The caretaker was a man called Joe Shields, who was a wonderful tinsmith. No matter what you wanted, a kettle, a back can or a bucket, he would have one made for you in a couple of hours. There was no charge for admission until around 1923 when they started asking sixpence, which was divided three ways – tuppence for the care-taker, tuppence for Darlington Memorial Hospital and tuppence for another hospital in Middlesbrough. The owners got nothing.

Around 1936, the North Region of the BBC did a radio programme about the legend of Mary, Queen of Scots, escaping from the castle and getting caught because she left her shawl on a thornbush up above Leyburn as she fled. Wilfred Pickles played the part of the gateman who was said to be bribed to let her go out and supposedly search for her ring. They put it out on *Children's Hour* and I've often thought about writing to the BBC to see if they still have a copy, because I would really like to hear it again.

Sadly, Roland Parker became a widower in 1988. But even though he is approaching eighty he is a very fit man, which is hardly surprising after all those years swinging a 16 lb hammer (which, by the way, he still has at the back of his post office, kept clean and ready just in case!). And he is obviously content, running the post office and selling small Wensleydale cheeses to the visitors. And keeping the place just as it was in the good old days when he was a youngster. Long may it remain so – indeed, I wish someone would issue a Preservation Order to maintain it just as it is for ever.

17

The Cockfield Choir –
My All-time Favourites

*T*hose of you who saw me 'dropped on' by *This is Your Life*, an honour I'd never envisaged, may recall that the programme was rounded off by a group of gentlemen, mostly elderly, who sang to me. They were the Cockfield Methodist Male Voice Choir, and I thought it was the perfect conclusion to a memorable occasion because they have been my favourites since I was a young girl. I would go anywhere, anytime to hear them.

During the last couple of years I have got to know them really well, and they have been kind enough to invite me, and even asked me to say a few words, at their 'Pleasant Hours' – the name they call the concerts they have given frequently over the years in the Darlington and Teesdale areas. They have been famous around these parts since before the Second World War to my knowledge, and it was during my school days that I first heard them. They came to the anniversary services at the Methodist Chapel in Baldersdale, led by a grand gentleman called George Tallentire Dickinson, who was related to me on the Tallentire side. He made several visits to our Dale, and I well recall him bringing a small concert party during the war, including Mr Edwin Coates who now leads the choir and plays the accordion. Edwin was in the RAF at the time but would give up his precious leave to come and sing and play for us. They brought musical instruments, including a violin, and also did marvellous monologues. Not all the songs were sacred pieces either – they had a wide repertoire of popular songs like 'Galway Bay', and their harmony was a treat for the ears. The choir naturally expanded after the war when the younger men came back home, and I heard them once or twice again, but the opportunities to go and see them were very limited for me then. I would read

Edwin and Jack Coates,
outside the chapel where
it all started.

about them in the *Teesdale Mercury* and wish for a chance to see and hear them more often.

But there was to be a remarkable turn of events. One day, some time after *Too Long A Winter* was shown, a knock came at the door at Low Birk Hatt and who should be standing there but Edwin Coates! Let him tell you the rest of the story.

It was just after the first programme which made such an impression around here when some friends called and asked if my wife and myself would like to try and visit Hannah, because they thought they knew whereabouts she lived.

So we went to the top of Baldersdale, ditched the cars and started walking across the fields. I went on ahead and knocked on this farmhouse door, which we had guessed was the right one, and sure enough Hannah appeared. I began to explain that she wouldn't know us, because we were from Cockfield, and she exclaimed, 'Oh, yes I do!' and immediately invited us in. Then she explained how she had attended our concert party during the war when she came to the chapel in Baldersdale, when I was on leave. She was even able to tell me the things that I had said on that occasion, the songs we had sung, even recalled my solo in detail. I was quite taken aback, I can tell you. All those years ago, and Hannah remembered everything to a tee! Now, that visit to Low Birk Hatt was something I will always remember, and so will the others in the party. We gathered round her organ, played and sang some hymns. That instrument was a bit difficult to get going, and someone had to push my backside so the seat wouldn't slip on the mat as I worked hard to get some pressure on the pedals. But Hannah stood by listening, with such a smile on her face, and said, 'I never thought the day would come when you, Edwin Coates, would play this organ!' So I replied, 'Miss Hauxwell, you are the famous one, not me.' I went back a second time and took my accordion to serenade her. Since then she has kindly consented to appear at our concerts on several occasions, and the audiences just love her.

The history of the choir goes back nearly seventy years – it is difficult to put your finger on it, but it all began when the late George Dickinson, my wife's uncle who was a local JP and councillor, called together the members of the Cockfield Methodist Church and said

The men of Cockfield Methodist Chapel, 1928.

168

(*top*) The original Cockfield Methodist Male Voice Choir, 1951. Edwin (*white handkerchief*) in the centre, Jack on the far right.
(*middle*) In 1953 – Edwin in the centre, Jack fourth from right.
(*bottom*) An appreciative audience of one, 1979.

The Cockfield Choir in 1992 . . .

we should put on a concert. That was in the 1920s. Cockfield is an old mining village in between Barnard Castle and Bishop Auckland. My father was a miner, but neither I nor my elder brother, Jack, followed him and the pit closed down a long time ago. We had a thriving chapel with fifty or sixty men attending regularly, and there was a surprising amount of musical talent in the village. We had a piano at home, and in our young days, long before television came along, we made our own entertainment. Father sang tenor, Jack sang bass, and one sister, Sylvia, was a soprano and the other, Annie, was a contralto. I sang alto, and Mother played the piano.

Anyway, the concert was very successful and it never stopped from then on. We got invitations to appear around the area, which became a problem during the war because of petrol rationing – we used to travel packed into cars. But certain arrangements were made because people were so keen for a bit of entertainment. There was a particular garage on the A1 where we could fill up, and that's how we were paid. I assume those wanting us to appear at their place would donate their precious petrol coupons.

I got the idea to run what we call the 'Pleasant Hour'. I was sent to Arbroath in Scotland on a course when I was in the RAF, and went

... with their most loyal supporter.

to an after-church gathering run by a man who would go round the audience asking people to sing or recite. He obviously knew, or suspected, that certain people were good at one or the other and it was impressive. Some were obviously beginners, but a remarkable number had real talent, and everyone was equally appreciated. So I came back to Cockfield and adapted the idea. I didn't go round the congregation, but divided the village into geographical areas, gave them fancy names and asked them to get together and organize a contribution of some sort or another.

Right from the start it all went remarkably well. You must remember that in those days women were not even allowed, never mind encouraged, to go into pubs and clubs, and there was another incentive – tea and biscuits. That was a rare treat, because tea was still rationed long after the war finished, and biscuits very hard to come by.

And it was open to everyone, whether or not they could sing, but they all wanted to try – people love to sing – and fifty people would turn up every Sunday evening. That's how the 'Pleasant Hour' started. The nucleus of course, was the Cockfield Methodist Male Voice Choir, which by 1951 had a uniform set of clothes and bow ties. It's rather sad now to look at the photographs we had taken that year because my brother Jack and I are the only ones still surviving. I'm approaching eighty myself, and Jack is seven years my senior! Together we have over a hundred years of service as accredited Methodist local preachers.

Obviously, there have been some changes to the choir over the years, and about half of the members now are retired gentlemen. But the Cockfield Methodist Male Voice Choir still goes on and so does the 'Pleasant Hour'. In recent times we have visited the North Shields Studios of BBC Radio on three occasions to record songs in the form of cassette tapes. As a result we have often been broadcast on the Frank Wappett Sunday morning service on Radio Newcastle.

Personally, I am so pleased that they have left something for posterity, as they have spread so much pleasure and happiness around the Teesdale area for so many years. They deserve much wider recognition, and I was so pleased to see them appearing at last on television when they featured me on *This Is Your Life*.

But they were so nervous on that occasion – it was somewhat overwhelming for everyone concerned – and didn't have much of a chance in the limited time available to display their wonderful talent properly. I hope another opportunity of a national audience will come their way. Like me, they are basically simple country folk. Two of them had never been to London before, and one of them announced it was also the first time he had ever been away from his wife, the first time he had spent the night in a hotel – and he was very worried because his wife had been left in sole charge of a hundred sheep and a bed-tempered ram!

I repeat – I would travel anywhere, anytime to hear the Cockfield Choir.

18

Jack Robinson and Yorkshire Day

*M*y northern journey now returns to the heart of Teesdale, my homeland. At the beginning of this book I stated that I believe myself to be the essential northerner, a Daleswoman through and through. More than that, even . . . for I am a *Yorkshire* Daleswoman. Now, for centuries people in Teesdale knew exactly where they were and who they were. The River Tees is the ancient border. South you have Yorkshire, to the north it is Durham. Baldersdale and Cotherstone are on the south side of the river so they are in Yorkshire, and as far as I am concerned always will be. But now a large slice of the south, including Low Birk Hatt Farm and Belle Vue Cottage are officially part of Durham. Now I am definitely not in agreement with changing the names of counties, or even houses come to that, if they have existed for donkeys' years. It is just not acceptable that someone in a London office with nothing to do one afternoon has a rush of blood to the head and begins redrawing old and accepted boundaries. I have nothing against Durham, but it was such a simple thing to understand when the Tees was the dividing line. It's daft . . . a politician's blunder with no advantage to anyone, as far as I know.

Now there's one man – a Yorkshire man, of course – who feels very deeply about all this and has made a wonderfully humorous and telling stand against it. He is Jack Robinson, the landlord of the Rose and Crown in Mickleton, just a few miles down the road from where I live. A very clever man who writes poetry and songs and raises lots of money for charity. There is a sign outside his pub saying, 'Welcome to Yorkshire', although officially it should say Durham, and he organizes a big celebration each year for Yorkshire Day, which happens to be my birthday, 1 August. I didn't even know there was such a thing as Yorkshire Day until he turned up at Low Birk Hatt one day, with Norman, my late cousin who lived just across the road from Jack. And I realized yet

again that I had discovered another blood relative! Our great-grand-fathers were brothers, so that makes us about quarter cousins. Then he invited me to help him celebrate Yorkshire Day in 1984, and wrote a song in my honour. I have been going ever since, and wouldn't miss it for anything. As you might imagine, he tells a good story.

With 'cousin' Jack Robinson, outside the Rose and Crown, Mickleton.

I was born myself in Otley, Yorkshire, in January 1928 – which makes me almost exactly eighteen months younger than Hannah. My grandmother was born at New Houses in Baldersdale, the daughter of James and Sarah Bayles. James was the fourth son of John Bayles, and Hannah's great-grandfather was the second son. I once said jokingly to a newspaper reporter that Hannah and I were thirty-second cousins and she took me up on this. She said that she had been thinking a lot about the matter and had worked out that since we were the same generation of the descendants that it should make us quarter cousins. In fact she pointed out when we all came down to London to appear on *This Is Your Life* that I was the only blood relative there! When I first met her at Low Birk Hatt she immediately accepted my invitation to Yorkshire Day and I asked her to put it down on her calendar. But the calendar was two years out of date, so she wrote it down on an old shoebox saying she wouldn't forget it as it was her birthday. That was in 1984, the first Yorkshire Day I ever organized, and she has been a regular ever since.

The *Northern Echo* wrote a story in advance of the first do, written by my pal, Mike Amos and, when it was announced that Hannah was coming, the television crews arrived. Three of them, Yorkshire Television, Tyne Tees Television and the BBC. She's always late, you know. I send a car for her, same driver every year. Once she announced through the letter-box that, although she'd had her bath, she still had to finish sewing the dress that she was making for the event. So he waited on the doorstep as she sat in her underwear, giving occasional progress reports via the letter-box!

I have written several songs, including two for Hannah – 'The Story of Hannah' and 'The Fields of Low Birk Hatt'. I write a new verse for the latter song each year to mark her birthday. In 1991, when she was sixty-five, it went:

> *But Hannah's here today, and we would like to say*
> *Happy Birthday Hannah, sixty-five*
> *May you live the life you want in any way you want*
> *With memories of Birk Hatt still alive.*

A White Rose cake with an appropriate message.

1 August became Yorkshire Day because of the Battle of Minden, fought on that day against the French. Many of the English troops were Yorkshiremen and they wore white roses, plucked from the hedgerows. And the King's Own Yorkshire Light Infantry celebrated the occasion every 1 August from then on, all ranks wearing a white rose and the sergeants waiting on the lower ranks in the mess halls like other regiments do on Christmas Day.

At the Rose and Crown, Yorkshire Day starts at 11.30 a.m., with the Yorkshire Flag flying outside and plenty of white roses around. Then I read out the Declaration of Integrity which goes like this:

> *I, Jack Robinson, being a native of Yorkshire and resident in Mickleton in the North Riding of Yorkshire, declare:*
>
> *That Yorkshire is three Ridings and the city of York with these boundaries which are 1,113 years standing.*
>
> *That the address of all places in these Ridings is Yorkshire.*
>
> *That all persons born therein or resident therein and loyal to the Ridings are Yorkshire men and women.*
>
> *That any person or corporate body which knavishly ignores or denies the above shall be outcast and unfit for the company of civilized men and women.*
>
> *These declarations made this Yorkshire Day.*
>
> *Yorkshire for ever.*
>
> *God save the Queen!*

Then I tell jokes, sing my songs, and we all have a few pints. When I start up with Ilkley Moor, that's the signal to bring the Yorkshire Puddings on. Plenty of 'em, with onion gravy and good Yorkshire parkin – that's like gingerbread, only better. And after we have all eaten I sing 'The Fields of Low Birk Hatt' and wish Hannah many happy returns. She sits at the bar with orange juice, smiling that smile of hers. When word got out that she had promised to attend, all our rooms were booked immediately. The place is usually full to the brim all day, and I do concede that a fair proportion of them come because of her. But it's all in a good cause, and not just to support the honour of Yorkshire. I have produced two booklets to go with the event – the first one sold out and the second one is likely to do the same. They contain my songs, stories, jokes and a few pearls of wisdom. I do go on a bit about the terrible injustice done to England's finest county. I mean, Mickleton had been part of Yorkshire ever since the Danes created the Ridings in the ninth century, but they just chopped it off the map when the boundaries were

(*left*) Jack Robinson in full flow.
(*right*) Signing session in the Rose and Crown.

changed in 1974. And I bring the attention of those responsible for this iniquitous act to the words of the Bible, Proverbs, Chapter 23, verses 10 and 11.

> *Do not move the ancient boundary stone, or encroach on land of orphans.*
> *They have a powerful Guardian, who shall take up their cause against you.*

And from the same book, Chapter 22, Verse 1:

> *A good name is more to be desired than riches.*
> *Esteem is better than silver or gold.*

The really good thing about Yorkshire Day and the booklets, apart from the fun we all have, is the money we raise for charity. When I celebrated my silver jubilee as a holder of a Justice's Licence, I was able to give £1,000 to the Guide Dogs for the Blind Association, and £300 to the local hospital.

I hope to raise a lot more on future Yorkshire Days.

19

The Bard of Teesdale and his Legacy

*T*he beauty of Teesdale has inspired many artists down the years and none more so than Richard Watson, a poor lead miner who lived in the nineteenth century and wrote such wonderful poetry that he became known as the Bard of Teesdale. In a sense, Richard Watson still lives, because during the last few years he has directly inspired two remarkable men in Teesdale to blossom as true artists. One is a painter, the other a wood carver, and I have come to know them both rather well.

Rob Bottomley is the painter, and he really got under the skin of Richard Watson – by playing the man himself in a drama written by my good friend, Jim McTaggart, the editor of the *Teesdale Mercury*. Rob then painted a landscape which included a portrait of the Teesdale Bard, which was his first serious work, although he had shown artistic talent since childhood. This led, with the help of a loyal wife, to a full-time and thankfully very successful career as an artist. He has done a portrait of me which I admire very much. Now, I have sat for several artists since I was brought to the attention of the public and all of them are good in their own way, but Rob's the best in my humble opinion.

The man himself has had such a fascinating life. He was the son of a Yorkshire miner who left school at the age of fifteen to follow his father down the pit. He stuck it until he was sixteen, then he walked out, in the middle of a shift. He had shown some talent for art at school, and was spotted by an inspector who toured schools specifically to examine creative work and encourage any potential pupils. This inspector was sufficiently impressed to turn up at Rob's home and urge his mother to think about sending him to art school. This advice was eventually followed, but he did not attend for very long – as he will tell you.

With Philip Townsend at his six panel, hand carved memorial to Richard Watson, in the centre of Middleton-in-Teesdale.

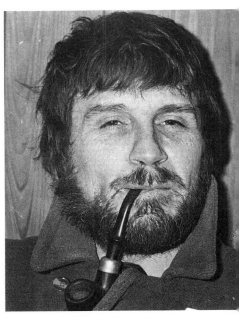

(*above*) Rob Bottomley,
playing the part of the
Bard in the play, 'Around
the Hollow Hills', by Jim
McTaggart.

(*left*) Richard Watson, the
Bard of Teesdale.

Around half an hour, as a matter of fact. Mother persuaded me to en-
rol at Doncaster Art School after I quit the pit, but I was a restless lad
and I ended up signing on for six years with the Coldstream Guards. I
had a terrible shock when I turned up at Caterham Barracks in 1958,
the first time in my life away from my mum's apron strings. I was
yelled at the moment I stepped through the gates, and my first night's
sleep was disturbed by the sobbing of other recruits. It was a tough
course – the discipline was really severe. The padre called, and I asked
him how was it that they could do it – treat you like dirt and call your
parents every name under the sun. He said it was the way of the army,
and you had to try and stick it out.

I decided to do just that. Admitting failure and going back home was unthinkable. But around a third of the lads on basic training with me couldn't take it and left. I then became what they call a trained soldier, and that was the start of growing up to become a man. They sent me to serve in Kenya and in South America, and the experience was wonderful. I also did two years guarding Buckingham Palace, pounding around with a bearskin on my head and everything.

Those six years were packed with incident. I really lived. There were some hairy moments, such as the time we were involved with riots in British Guyana, and some very funny ones, too. The most hilarious happened outside Buckingham Palace when an officer was trying to give the order to fix bayonets during the changing of the guard, on a very hot summer's day. He had a stammer, and couldn't get out the word bayonet. He went on and on, with everyone half dead with the heat and trying like hell to avoid laughing. It finally proved too much for one of the guardsmen, who collapsed to his knees, bearskin flying off and rifle crashing to the ground. He was helpless, in agony almost, yelling with laughter. The RSM went purple with rage and screamed, 'Get that man!' and two large corporals dragged him off to the guardroom. He got twenty-eight days, but later told me it was worth it.

When I came out of the army I worked at Butlin's on security, which meant I wore a blue coat instead of a red one. Eventually, I ended up in Teesdale with my wife, Rose, after one unsuccessful marriage. I did some painting and decorating and we ran a bed-and-breakfast establishment. I also did a little art, but nothing to speak of. Then Rose, who had made her name in the clubs as a singer, staged *The Boyfriend* for a local amateur society and cast me as a lead. Then up came Jim McTaggart with his play about Richard Watson, based on his book, *Around the Hollow Hills*, saying he wanted Rose to produce it, and me to play the title role. I was so impressed by his story. Richard was a lead miner with eight daughters who had a tremendous talent and did something about it, enduring hardship to succeed. I decided that if he could do it then I should try too. Rose gallantly took a job on the factory line at Glaxo to enable me to become a real painter. I started, fittingly, with a portrait of Richard Watson, placed in a landscape. It was hard at first, particularly for Rose, and then things took off financially. I landed a commission for £5,000, sold three more for a total of £8,000 and opened a gallery in Barnard Castle. It's been a dream.

I first met Hannah when she turned up with Jim McTaggart at the

Rob, the artist, with his subject.

first night of the Richard Watson production, and I will never forget the incredible impression she created. All the young men in the company were enthralled by the serenity and gentleness of this woman. So I did her portrait from a photograph. I put it in the window of my gallery and it drew so many crowds that we decided to issue a print, with part of the proceeds going to charity. Eventually, I want to do a full-length portrait in that old coat, with the wellies, a stick, dog and maybe the shadow of a film crew in the snow!

The other artist who found inspiration from Richard Watson is Phillip Townsend who has the remarkable ability to carve portraits in wood – not a common art form. He was born in Leicester and came to Middleton-in-Teesdale in 1989 after spending some years with his wife and family in Donegal, where he had a successful business in a craft village making wooden bowls, clocks and similar objects for the tourist trade. He is a skilled maker of furniture and has a design degree. His wife, Audrey, paints very attractive watercolours. They hoped to be part of a Heritage and Craft centre, combined with a Tourist Information Office, in Middleton, but the District Council sadly shelved that plan. His major work up to now has been a full-length, life-size, deep-relief carving of the Queen Mother when she was the Lady Elizabeth Bowes Lyon at the age of twenty-one. It is exceedingly good, and was done to celebrate the centenary of the Bowes Museum in Barnard Castle, which was built by her ancestors. And the man, bless him, has carved a likeness of me.

(*Overleaf*) (*left*) An exterior view of Philip Townsend's workshop.

(*right*) Working on a certain portrait . . . of me!

I met Hannah in 1990 after doing a relief carving of her taken from a photograph, from *Seasons of My Life*, I believe. I brought it to show her – it seemed only polite as it was to be displayed in the local town. I have a warm memory of that first visit to her house in Cotherstone – the gentle, unhurried, ever-courteous reception she gave to me, a complete stranger, and the way her hands stroked and fluttered over the surface of the carving in appreciation. It was, in fact, one of the very first carvings I had done, having taken up the craft partly because I'd had a set of carving tools for years and always promised myself I would see what could be done with them one day, and partly because my capacity for making furniture was limited by the size of the workshop-cum-garage I now have.

Last year was the centenary of the death of Richard Watson. When he died, a fund was begun for a memorial but it came to nothing, due to lack of support. In an attempt to put this to rights, I designed a six-panel memorial which now fills a large window in

the centre of Middleton-in-Teesdale. The centrepiece is a carving of Watson himself, while the surrounding panels are illustrations of names and places connected with his life, and an extract from his poems and brief life history – all done with a technique known as pyrography, using a red hot wire burning into the wood.

When the memorial was officially unveiled it was Hannah who graciously did the honours, despite a very full diary at the time. The big turnout for the occasion was, I suspect, due far more to her presence than any interest in our long-dead poet. Hannah herself is a genuine fan of his work, and can readily quote several of his poems. It's worth remarking that when all the hullaballoo was over she was the last one there at the window, still intently reading what most simply glossed over.

I thought it would be fitting to end this chapter with some verse by Richard Watson himself, the man who has given such pleasure to me, to many generations before me, and I am sure, will do the same for many more to come.

The Teesdale Hills

I've wandered many a weary mile,
And in strange countries been,
I've dwelt in towns and on wild moors,
And curious sights I've seen;
But still my heart clings to the dale,
Where Tees rolls to the sea,
Compared with what I've seen I'll say,
The Teesdale hills for me.

Let minstrels sing till they are hoarse,
Of Scotia's woods and dells,
And winding streams and mountains steep,
Where bloom sweet heather bells,
Their strains still fail to touch my heart,
My fav'rite ones shall be
Those that remind me of my home,
The Teesdale hills for me.

RICHARD WATSON *(1833-1891)*

20

Good Neighbours and Old Skills

I will conclude this book where it all began – in Baldersdale. My heart still resides there, and all my fondest memories stem from the sixty-two years I spent there, all through the time when my family was still with me and the Dale had a thriving community, down the decades to the long years I spent on my own and Baldersdale gradually emptied.

Farming is a good and satisfying life, but never easy. We all knew hard times in Baldersdale because it is not a generous place, and sometimes the fight to survive became almost unbearable, particularly when the weather damaged the vital hay crop or the winter storms came at lambing time. But there was a spirit in Baldersdale which lifted you up when all seemed lost. Unfailingly, there would be someone to come to your rescue, without even being asked. No one was ever abandoned. Neighbours would know instinctively when someone was in dire trouble and through the gate they would come, shovels and rakes at the ready.

The Hauxwells had cause to be thankful to several families in the dale, and we did our best to return favours when we were able. I particularly recall with much fondness the kindness of the Fawcetts at West Birk Hatt, the Thwaites of High Birk Hatt and, more recently, the friends who farmed Clove Lodge, which is perched on the hill above Low Birk Hatt. First there was the Hind family, who would invite me to share Christmas with them, and they were followed by Mr and Mrs Maurice Atkinson, who were always ready to assist when one was in need. When the major portion of my somewhat meagre income in the pre-television era came from the sale of the single calf I had bred each year, Maurice would take it to the auction mart for me, organizing everything. I was so sad when ill health obliged Maurice to leave, and I thought it might not be possible for the gap to be filled.

A view of Low Birk Hatt from a position near Clove Lodge.

I was wrong. For along came Bill Purves, who arrived in 1984 with his wife and their two daughters. They came from an unusual background – not farming stock at all. Bill was a seafaring man and an engineer for many years and came into farming with no experience at all. He ran a milk farm with real flair, despite difficulties created by bureaucracy, before coming to Clove Lodge. Now he has a flock of five hundred sheep on the piece of fell that goes with the property, and a few beef cattle.

I liked him the first moment I saw him, and he has done so much for me that I will always be grateful to him.

I can't quite recall the first time I met Hannah, but I do remember seeing this figure in the far distance going down, stick in hand, to the reservoir, to fill up a gallon can – backwards and forwards all day. It was a very dry summer, and I went down to see if I could help. I had a 200-gallon bowser on the back of my tractor so I took it to the youth hostel and filled it up there, where they had pure drinking water. And I placed the bowser up against her back door and showed her how to open and shut the valve. It kept her going a

Bill Purves, with one of his dogs, outside Clove Lodge.

good long while.

A bit later a very strange thing happened. We had this little field at the bottom of our spread, fairly close to Low Birk Hatt, which had been cut for hay. It was the last of the hay we had that year. The grass had been turned a few times but the ground was too wet to pick it up. We got the baler in eventually, but it got bogged down and in the end we decided to scrap it – just leave the grass where it was.

I got on with dosing some sheep for worms, worked all day at that, and in the late afternoon I glanced down at that lower field and saw a pole going up and down behind the wall. I was too busy to go and investigate, but I kept seeing the pole popping up and wondered what the heck could be happening. Anyway, I finished around tea-time, went down and discovered that Hannah had hand-raked the grass into a stook. She was walking round and round it, heaping more on and it stood about five foot high. I couldn't understand why she was doing this because I thought the stuff was rubbish. Then she said she would top it off. She had this special method, an old-fashioned way of doing it which was almost like thatching. She actually made two ricks like that, and just one takes all day.

I did ask her to please not waste her time on it because I had already decided to scrap it, but she told me quite firmly that she wasn't going to see good hay like that get lost. So I left her to it.

Do you know, the hay that came off those ricks was perfect. We had a full winter on it, and it was really sweet. Obviously, she had some kind of old skill.

The following year Margaret and I worked baling hay until dark and we left some bales on the ground. Now you really should stook bales to stop rain damaging them and there had been a patchy forecast but we had had enough that day. Next morning I went down and all the bales had been stacked, two or three bales high. I was mystified at first, and then I guessed. Hannah!

She had worked through the night. Although it never really gets dark on summer nights in Baldersdale, that lady must have the eyesight of an owl!

Well, I did what I could to help. Bill and Margaret had obviously had a long hard day, so I stacked the bales to protect them from the rain. They are such good people, and Bill has done marvellously well with Clove Lodge.

He is the man who agreed to look after Rosa and my other cattle when I left Baldersdale, and he has given them a good home ever since. That is so important because, although they may be dumb beasts, they are very special to me. Particularly Rosa, the mother cow. He has cared for her through a rather nasty bout of mastitis. Patch has also been ill with bad do of the staggers, but she recovered so well that afterwards she even had a calf. Bill is still doing me favours, giving me advice on property maintenance and the like, and keeping me well informed about the beasties.

He's a grand man. As long as there are people like him and Margaret around, the old spirit of Baldersdale will survive.

With my good friend Bill, in Baldersdale.

190